GREAT EXPLORERS

Endpapers: Victoria Falls with Stampeding Buffaloes, painted by Thomas Baines, who was with Livingstone when he visited the Falls in 1862.

Above: A medieval manuscript illumination from Marco Polo's *Livre de Merveilles,* showing sailing ships navigating the waters near the Andaman Islands.

Overleaf: The War Boats of the Island of Otaheite and the Society Isles, by William Hodges, draughtsman on Captain Cook's second voyage, 1772–5.

Contents pages: Blizzard conditions in the Arctic.

GREAT EXPLORERS

Roderic Owen

MAYFLOWER BOOKS
NEW YORK

Library of Congress Cataloging in Publication Data
Owen, Roderic
Great Explorers

ISBN: 0 8317 3969 X
MANUFACTURED IN ITALY
FIRST AMERICAN EDITION

Contents

Origins

It is providential that men's curiosity is boundless, for from earliest times they have needed to be explorers. When hunting grounds became overcrowded, or when lands became uninhabitable through natural disasters, they needed to find new lands to support them. Before the time of any of the explorers in this book men already inhabited even the inhospitable parts of every continent except the polar regions. And wherever later explorers went, they nearly always found developed civilizations to greet them.

Over the centuries the motives for exploration have changed only a little: trade, especially for exotic merchandise, has always been a paramount reason, and hand-in-hand with it, particularly on the part of European Christians, has gone a missionary zeal to convert the heathen. The desire for gain – of personal riches or colonies for the explorer's native land, or of personal or national glory – has also prompted many explorers to venture into unknown regions; and sheer curiosity, or an interest in scientific enquiry, particularly in recent years, has prompted spectacular voyages of discovery.

One cannot escape the feeling that much modern exploration, from conquering Everest to crossing oceans on unsuitable craft, is a deliberately contrived exercise. Technology threatens gradually to thrust exploration into a new category: radio communications, for instance, so transform a journey into the unknown that comparison with past experience is virtually impossible. How can the trials of a twentieth-century man who has only to press a button to be in instant contact with his fellows be compared with the feats of endurance of the past? New drugs, too, have altered the terms on which explorers maintain their health, even their lives. It was the work of scientists in the early years of *this* century which led to the isolation of vitamin C and its eventual synthesis; and not until then could scurvy, the bane of so many explorers, be effectively contained under all conditions.

However, even sophisticated technology cannot be entirely reliable, and when it goes wrong the results can be disastrous. It is at that point that greatness still counts. Explorers are often accused of wishing to test themselves rather than their environment. If that is really the stimulus they require, then we should let them have it; for the rest of us are enriched at second hand by their experiences.

A few of the great explorers of recorded history figure in these pages. Many more names are missing because there is no room to give them the consideration they deserve. The lives of all of them show what could be done, and against what odds, by brave men, as hard on themselves as on others, who knew what fear was, but who would rather die than give in.

Opposite The four thousand-year-old temple of the Egyptian Queen Hatshepsut at Deir-el-Bahri.

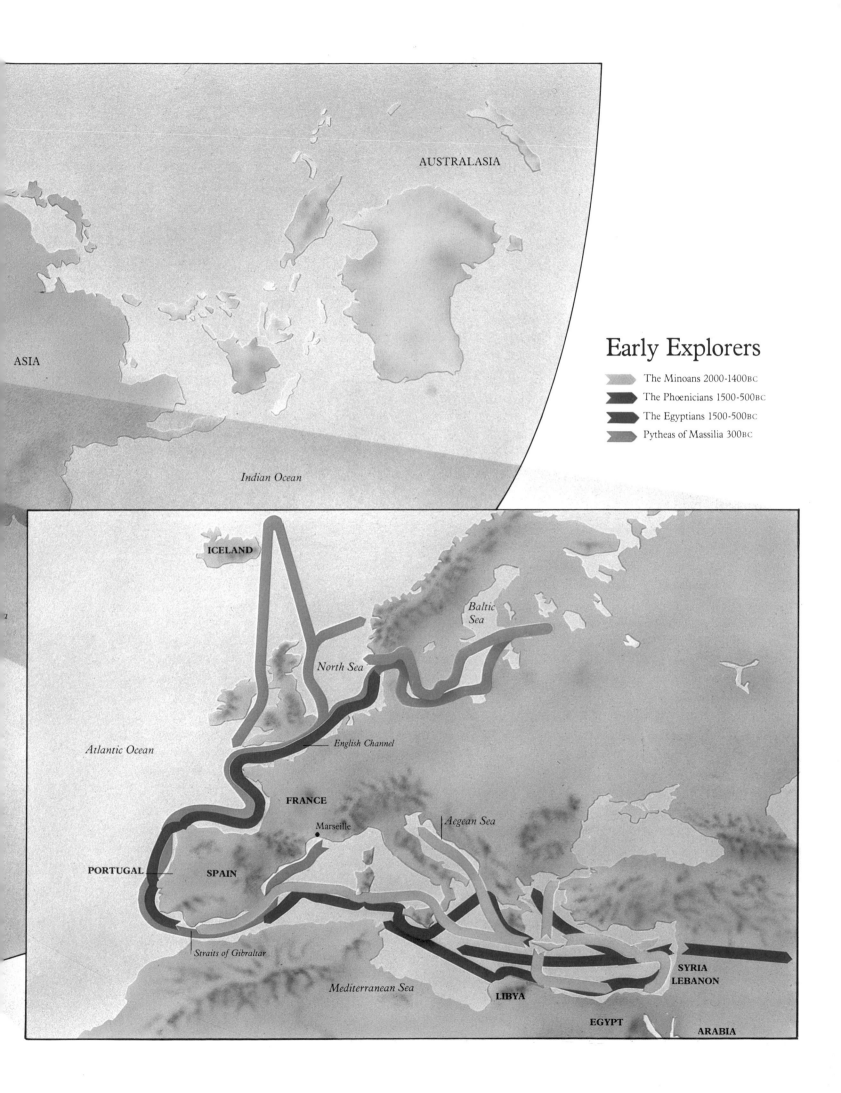

Early Explorers

The Minoans 2000-1400BC

The Phoenicians 1500-500BC

The Egyptians 1500-500BC

Pytheas of Massilia 300BC

AUSTRALASIA

ASIA

Indian Ocean

ICELAND

Baltic Sea

North Sea

Atlantic Ocean

English Channel

FRANCE

Marseille

Aegean Sea

PORTUGAL   SPAIN

Straits of Gibraltar

Mediterranean Sea

LIBYA

SYRIA
LEBANON

EGYPT

ARABIA

Ten thousand years before Christ some of the agriculturalists of the Mediterranean basin settled in what is known as the Fertile Crescent, an area curving from the top of the Persian Gulf – Ur of the Chaldees and Babylon, via Nineveh and Haran (Mesopotamia and Syria) to Carchemish, Tyre and Shechem (Nablus). Here they created cities whose function was to rule and to trade (the one often being an extension of the other) far south to the Indus Valley and beyond. In the cities water pipes gurgled and women decked themselves with jewels. The age of luxury had begun.

The first explorers to venture out from the Mediterranean-based civilizations, in the second century BC, were the Egyptians, the Minoan Cretans, and the Phoenicians. Because of records kept by Egyptians, whose Nile-based civilization was the wonder of their own and succeeding ages, it can be proved that Thutmosis III was supplied with wood from the Lebanon by Cretan contractors, in a typical business deal of the day. During Thutmosis' minority his mother-in-law, Queen Hatshepsut, acted as regent. Her ships were active further to the south, and she can be regarded as one of the earliest promoters of exploration. Frescoes and sculpted inscriptions on the wall of her temple at Deir-el-Bahri give an account of an expedition sent down the Red Sea in the direction of Somalia in about 1492 BC, on the direct orders, she said, of the god Amun-Ra, who described in detail the 'ladders of incense' that the exploring traders were to find in the land of Punt. The inhabitants of Punt asked the newcomers, to their gratification, whether they had sailed in their five ships down from the sky. Feasts were duly given on both sides and trade in the much-desired incense in the form of woods and resins, and various outlandish products such as monkey skins, even a live panther, proceeded apace. No one can be quite sure of the exact location of Punt; it may have been southern Arabia, or anywhere down the east African coast as far as Mozambique. In any case, the Egyptians would have had to negotiate 1500 miles of the shark-infested and treacherous waters of the Red Sea and the Arabian Sea.

After such a brilliant venture, Egyptian traders continued to be active in the Red Sea, using Phoenician sailors if necessary. The historian Herodotus, who was himself an explorer-traveller, recorded that King Necho II (610–595 BC) decided to stop building a canal between the Nile and the Arabian Gulf and instead sent a number of ships manned by Phoenicians, with orders to make for the Pillars of Hercules (Straits of Gibraltar) and return to Egypt through them and by the Mediterranean.

The sailors duly left Egypt via the Red Sea. They were prepared to live off the land; having provided themselves with seed-corn, they sowed it in the autumn wherever they happened to be, waited to reap a crop, and moved on again. It apparently took three years before they reappeared in the Mediterranean; and their story of the circumnavigation of an immense Africa stretching far to the south was treated with some scepticism. Herodotus, writing over a hundred years later, reported: 'On their return they said – others may believe them, but I do not – that they had the sun on their right hand when sailing round Libya.' Then as now, travellers' tales were likely to be taken with a pinch of salt. However, it was lucky for Necho's men that Herodotus made that comment, for it proved that they had indeed been far into the southern hemisphere.

Before the heyday of Egyptian maritime expeditions the Minoans, based in Crete, had been the greatest explorers of the Mediterranean. The Minoans traded with Egypt, with islands throughout the Aegean, and with Mediterranean countries as far west as Spain, before their whole culture disappeared in a mysterious cataclysm. When the volcanic island of Santorini erupted in about 1450 BC earthquakes and tidal waves caused a great flood in the Mediterranean which may have destroyed the Minoans. It may also have been the origin of the biblical account of the great flood whose currents swept Noah away for 150 days before an olive leaf fetched by a dove heralded unknown land. The excitement of finding land after an indefinitely long sea voyage cannot have changed throughout the centuries.

The Phoenicians, who had sailed with the Egyptians, continued to show exploring-trading enterprise. In 500 BC, Hanno of Carthage left the Mediterranean via the Straits of Gibraltar, with sixty ships of fifty oars and travelled south down the west coast of Africa, reaching some point beyond Sierra Leone and founding the cities of Mogador and Agadir and temples as he went. Beyond that he found 'inhospitable Ethiopians' (he was under the mistaken impression that any country which lay beyond Libya must be Ethiopia) then crocodiles and hippopotamuses in Senegal and Gambia. His journey ended when the expedition ran out of food at an

Below A painted limestone sphinx of Queen Hatshepsut from her temple at Deir-el-Bahri.

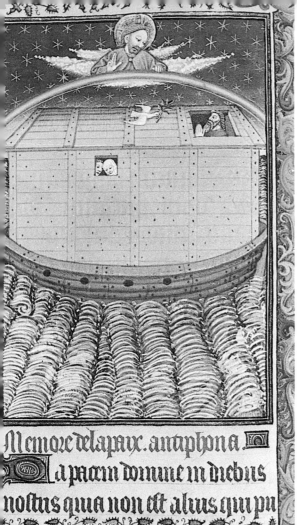

island 'full of wild people' (probably chimpanzees) covered in hair. When approached, the wild creatures fled, showering the explorers with stones, but three of the 'women' were captured, biting and scratching. They were duly killed and skinned and their hides were brought back in triumph to Carthage.

The Phoenicians were not content merely to probe southwards. Their galleys edged northwards round the coasts of France, Spain and Portugal to Britain. But the first historical account we have of ancient Britons comes from Pytheas, a scientifically-minded Greek from Massilia (Marseille), in about 300 BC. His original writings have vanished, but according to the accounts we have (third-hand versions by Pliny and Strabo), his was a private venture, unaided by the authorities. Before he left he fixed the exact latitude of his point of departure and decided which star nearest the pole to choose by which to navigate his course.

After a landfall in Cantion (Kent) Pytheas set out on foot for Belerion (Cornwall) to inspect the tin mines. 'The people were very hospitable, their converse with foreign merchants having civilized them and softened their manners.' Tin was apparently collected in a depot on Ictis (St

Left This miniature from a French illuminated manuscript of the early fifteenth century shows a fanciful depiction of Noah's Ark.

Below Assyrian oarsmen are the driving power of this galley, typical of the vessels used by the explorer-traders of the ancient world.

Michael's Mount) for trans-shipment by traders across the Channel and down the Rhône to Massilia.

It was Pytheas who reached, or at least described, Thule, presumably the Orkneys or Shetlands, a six-day voyage north from Scotland. In these forlorn regions he found that 'neither earth, water nor air exist separately, but a sort of concretion of all these in which the earth, sea and all things were suspended ... it can neither be travelled over nor sailed through' – an accurate description of freezing fog at the edge of slush ice.

Besides being an inventive practical astronomer, Pytheas was an expert on tidal ebbs and flows, and on much else besides. He observed how drinking habits changed the further north he went – wine gradually disappearing and its place being taken by honey mead. He was the first to describe beer, made from fermented barley, called *curmi*. He observed how 'in consequence of the rain and the absence of sun the [natives of Britain] did not use threshing floors, but threshed their corn in large barns'. It would have seemed highly unlikely to Pytheas that such beer-sodden and mead-soaked northerners would ever be in a position to compete with the developed civilizations of the Mediterranean. Indeed, much time would have to go by before such things began to occur; and then only after the Romans, successors to the Greeks, had pushed their empire to the limits of Pytheas's bold explorations.

Below St Magnus' Bay, Shetland, which the Greeks and Romans may well have considered to be *Ultima Thule*, the most northerly habitable spot on earth.

The Lure of the East

The Mediterranean Sea was the tiny centre around which flourished the ancient and medieval civilizations of Europe. The nature of the rest of the earth's surface was the subject of speculation, sometimes remarkably accurate and sometimes wildly fanciful. West of the Mediterranean lay vast seas; east lay a land of rich plains, forests and the mountains of northern India. The coasts of India were partly known, as they formed part of the ancient trading link between the coasts of the Mediterranean and Arabic Seas. Beyond lay China, the legendary Cathay, land of silks and spices.

Alexander the Great was the first to move out of familiar territory, not for reasons of trade, but out of unbounded ambition for power. His endless need for military conquest took him through vast areas of uncharted land, from the Caspian Sea across the mountains of the Hindu Kush to the Indus Valley, and then westwards across the desolate Iranian plateau to Susa. Fortunately he also had the consuming curiosity of the explorer for the new lands he was charting, and took scientists and mapmakers with him so that his discoveries could be documented and the new knowledge taken back home to Greece.

Hsüan-tsang followed, three centuries later, a Chinese Buddhist monk inspired by his passion for ideas to cross the parched wastes of the Gobi Desert and the icy peaks of the Hindu Kush in a search for pure, Sanskrit Buddhist texts. Chinese traders were, by comparison, slow to follow; indeed, considering the size and riches of the population, the Chinese took a long time to explore Europe, feeling that they had little to learn from 'foreign devils'.

By the middle ages the lure of the east was felt most strongly by traders eager for perfumes, silks and spices. Before the days of refrigeration meat quickly rotted; spices were essential for disguising the taste of tainted flesh. Hygiene and sanitation were primitive; and incense and perfumes disguised the smell of tainted air. And silk was a luxury fabric for which the demand was always greater than the supply. So, whilst the west hardly beckoned at all, the call of the Indies and Cathay was exotic merchandise.

The production of silk was a closely guarded secret of Cathay; but it was soon to become common knowledge. During the Emperor Justinian's reign (AD 527–65) silk-worm eggs were brought back to Constantinople in a hollow bamboo, perhaps by two monks. The Crusades provided a religious impetus to further commerce, delighting the merchants of Genoa and Venice. But the caravans still toiled slowly along trails thousands of miles long, constantly threatened with attack on the road, and stopping at the *serais*, the inns where traders could rest and lick their wounds.

The Polos, uncle, father and son, established a foothold in China in the thirteenth century. Their journeys by land and sea were some of the most fascinating in history. Very different from the wily Venetian traders was Ibn Battūta, the Muslim pilgrim and adventurer who went further than any other medieval traveller, journeying through Arabia, India, Southeast Asia and North Africa.

Nineteenth and twentieth-century explorers have been more scientifically motivated. In the fertile areas of land watered by the Mekong River, the jungle hid the Khmer civilization from human eye until in the mid-nineteenth century the French naturalist Mouhot stumbled across the fantastic ruins of Angkor, choked by invading trees. Mouhot was neither a standard bearer for commerce nor a flag waver. Explorers such as he were there to find out and report back their findings to European scientists and geographers.

Mouhot was only one of several to unearth buried eastern cities. Sven Hedin crossed and recrossed the Gobi Desert, often travelling by paths known to the earliest explorers, furthering their discoveries and helping to complete our knowledge of the Asian heartland.

Explorers of Asia

Alexander 334-23 BC
Hsüan-tsang 629-45
The Polos 1260-8
Marco Polo 1271-95
Ibn Battūta 1325-50
Ibn Battūta 1325-50 (return journey)
Mouhot 1858
Hedin 1893-1908

MONGOLIA

Peking

Turfan

Gobi Desert

Kucha

TIBET

CHINA

River Brahmaputra

River Ganges

River Mekong

Pacific Ocean

THAILAND
(SIAM)

Bangkok

Angkor

CAMBODIA

Phnom Penh

CEYLON

Singapore

Straits of
Malacca

SUMATRA

JAVA

Alexander the Great

(356 – 23 BC)

Alexander was a military genius, decisive, daring and ruthless, who used exploration to further his aims and a peculiarly enlightened form of administration to consolidate them. Clean-shaven in an age of beards, attractive to men and women alike, he became a god in his own lifetime.

He was born in 356 BC, the son of Philip II, king of Macedon (now northern Greece). His upbringing was influenced by the philosopher Aristotle, who taught him that the earth was round and that the world the Greeks knew was bounded by a great sea called Ocean, and inspired in him an interest in scientific matters and medicine as well as philosophy. This interest remained with Alexander during his years of military conquest and made him one of the first great explorers. He was driven not only by the desire for gain and victory, but also by simple curiosity and intellectual interest; for this reason his army included mathematicians, astronomers, geographers, architects, botanists and an official historian. Early in life Alexander had to be both governor and soldier, ruling the country at sixteen while the king was absent, and fighting at his father's side against the allied Greek states at Chaeronea two years later. When Philip was assassinated in 336 BC, the army gave Alexander its support and he succeeded unopposed.

Above A cameo of Alexander the Great and his mother, the 'weird, visionary and terrible' Olympias: disavowed by her husband, Philip of Macedon, then banished by her son.

Opposite 'Is it not passing brave to be a king And ride in triumph through Persepolis?' wrote Christopher Marlowe in *Tamburlaine*. Alexander sacked the great Persian city and, according to legend, Thais, an Athenian courtesan in Alexander's train, set fire to it during a drunken orgy.

To secure his throne he immediately had all possible pretenders put to death. When the only remaining obstacle was his mother, Olympias, he managed to arrange for her permanent retirement from public affairs. At the age of twenty, he was powerful – and he was alone.

Once free to deal with his inheritance, he set out to bind together a federation of Greek states under Macedonian control, subduing revolt with great severity. This done, he set out to realize an ambition which his father had had before him: to defeat the Persian emperor, Darius III, and conquer his vast empire. Thus it was that his desire for military glory led him, in 334, to cross the Dardanelles into Asia Minor, and on into territory previously unknown to the Greeks. Sardis, Ephesus, Miletus and Halicarnassus soon fell to his army of 35,000 men, and Alexander advanced upon Gordium, in Phrygia, with its famous knot. Whoever managed to untie the intricate Gordian knot, ran the prophecy, would be master of Asia. 'Who cares about untying it?' Alexander is supposed to have said – and promptly cut it.

On to Cilicia, Syria and Palestine he drove, inflicting defeat on the Persian forces at the battle of Issus (333) and capturing Darius' baggage train, and even his household.

His progress was checked briefly at Tyre but, after a siege of seven months, the city fell and its 30,000 inhabitants were sold into slavery as a reprisal. The way to Egypt was now clear, and he spent the winter of 332–1 there, founding Alexandria in the Nile delta and making the difficult journey to visit the oracle of the god Ammon in the Siwa Oasis, where he was hailed as the 'King of Kings', as any pharaoh would have been. The difference was that in Alexander's case it was to come true.

From Egypt he continued his pursuit of Darius, striking at the Persian-controlled

cities of the Fertile Crescent. Nineveh fell; and then, after the battle of Arbela, Babylon, whilst the Emperor Darius fled ever eastwards before him. Setting up civil administrations with shrewd clemency, Alexander headed for the treasuries of the Persians – the cities of Persis, Susa, Pasargadae and Persepolis.

The great city of Persepolis sat on an artificial platform at the foot of some low hills, not easy to defend against the apparently invincible Alexander. Its fall marked the end of the Achmaenid dynasty. Indeed its sacking became famous for something which probably never happened – the moment when Thais, an Athenian courtesan, was said to have reeled, shrieking, through the palace with a lighted firebrand, setting the place ablaze. The palace was set on fire and ten thousand manuscripts of the religious prophet Zoroaster were consumed in the flames – an irreparable loss.

As Alexander's forced marches carried his army eastwards he made use of the scientists and men of learning he had brought with him. He sent explorers out on subsidiary journeys. One of these, his admiral Nearchus, set sail in 325 to trace the east coast of the Persian Gulf. Afterwards Alexander was reputed to have said: 'Your success pleases me more than my whole conquest of Asia.' But the real success of Nearchus' journey of around twelve hundred miles lay in the minute attention to detail in the survey he made.

Alexander continued eastwards from Persepolis, across the Iranian plateau, to the Caspian Gates; he finally caught up with the Persian emperor to find him dying from wounds, and carried on to the Caspian Sea. Here the discovery that the Caspian contained no sea fish seemed to disprove the Greek theory that it was the point furthest south of a bay of Ocean extending into Asia from the north.

Above Alexander made a lasting impression upon India, where tribesmen in the Hindu Kush still claim descent from his soldiery. This miniature from a manuscript in the British Museum shows him with Roxane, whom he married at Balkh, thus cementing his alliance with powerful local chieftains.

Above Alexander meets the Brahmin in India. To his conquering zeal he added insatiable curiosity: he wished to meet and learn from every philosopher in the world.

With Persia at heel, the conquest of India could proceed apace. The Indian sub-continent south of the Indus was uncharted territory to Alexander and his soldiers. They believed Pakistan was a part of Egypt, bounded to the south of the Himalayas by the great Ocean. Through the valleys of the Hindu Kush in 328 and 327 Alexander pursued enemies who hurriedly became friends. Bactria and Sogdiana were soon pacified, and at Balkh, as an act of reconciliation, Alexander married Roxane, the daughter of a chieftain who had opposed him. Then, on he swept via the valleys of Swat and Dir. His storming of Aornos, which legend said that even Heracles had been unable to subdue, made such an impact that the Kalash Kafirs of Chitral and the people of Hunza and Nagir still claim that they are descended from the Macedonian soldiery.

In Taxila he rested to consolidate his gains; on the banks of the Jhelum he founded two cities – Alexandria Nicaea and Bucephala, the latter named after his horse,

Bucephalus, which died there. From Taxila he proceeded to the Punjab. There he demonstrated his impetuous bravery: jumping into the midst of the defenders of Malli in front of three companions, he was cut down and nearly died.

Alexander's progress eastward had now reached its furthest limit. His ambition, however, was not satisfied even by the vast journey he had already undertaken. He now announced to his exhausted army that he intended to march to the Ganges, 300 miles south-east, and sail down it to Ocean:

If any of you wish to know what limit may be set to this particular campaign, let me tell you that the area of country ahead of us, from here to the Ganges, is comparatively small. You will undoubtedly find that this ocean is connected with the Hyrcanian [Caspian] Sea, for the great stream of Ocean encircles the earth.

The reaction of his army was summed up by one of his generals: 'If there is one thing . . . that a successful man should know, it is *when to stop*.' So Alexander was forced to return westwards, sailing down the Jhelum to the mouth of the Indus on the Arabian Sea. Here, he divided his army into three. Part of the army embarked with Nearchus to sail along the coast of the Persian Gulf; their job was to find watering spots on a route which Alexander intended to be a shipping route from the Tigris to the Euphrates. Part, under Craterus, was to proceed to Salmons (Golashkerd), seventy miles inland from the Strait of Hormuz. The third part, under the command of Alexander, set off overland to cross the inhospitable deserts of the Makran coast, exploring the shore of the Arabian Sea and the Persian Gulf. The march to Pura took sixty days. In a seemingly endless sea of shifting sand dunes, they had to contend with sandstorms, quicksand, poisonous plants and snakes, and a flash flood which swept away all their baggage. The water ran out and wells were few and far between. In all 60,000 of the army were lost, as well as all the pack animals and baggage.

Nearchus meanwhile explored the Makran coast, finding various primitive peoples: hairy men who used their finger-nails for tools, and the Icthyophagi, fish-eaters, who lived entirely in and off fish products. They were also amazed to see whales, whose ribs the Icthyophagi used to make their huts.

By now, Alexander's Macedonian soldiers were weary of such endless military exploration. They had marched across mountains, waist-deep in snow, and suffer-ing frostbite, snow-blindness and the

effects of altitude; and they had marched across deserts under a blazing sun and put up with heatstroke, disease and thirst. Now they just wanted to go home, and Alexander faced a serious mutiny.

Alexander's reaction was to pour scorn on them: 'Go back home, then! Tell them you deserted your king in his hour of need!' When he said he would recruit Persians to replace the Macedonians, the men's resistance crumbled.

In 323 he moved to Babylon which he wanted to rehabilitate as a port, as he nurtured plans for the circumnavigation of Africa. Alexander had been warned that he would meet his fate in Babylon. Thus it was, one day in June, whilst they were celebrating the completion of his ship-building programme with a lengthy bout of drinking, Alexander became feverish. He took little notice and the fever seemed to abate, but ten days later it returned with redoubled force. Soon he was unable to speak; his anxious Macedonians, who had until then been kept at arm's length, were

now suffered to pass in front of their dying leader. They had no more than a day to take their last leave of him before the end came. Alexander, the god, the 'invincible', had been brought low by one of the humblest of all creatures; for his fever was presumably malarial, and malaria, as we now know, is spread by the bite of the female mosquito.

In the ten years since he had crossed the Hellespont into Asia Minor he had travelled, with his armies, over 20,000 miles through land known only sketchily to the Persians, and unknown to the Greeks. The empire he founded was vast, and spread the ideas of his native Macedonia and Greece throughout Europe and Asia Minor. Fortunately for Greek scholars, he was not just a brilliant military commander, for he ensured that whenever he passed through new territory records were made and specimens taken to add to the Greeks' sparse knowledge of the east.

Above The Bande Amir Lakes in Afghanistan, which Alexander swept past on his progress to the rich plains of India.

Hsüan-tsang

(*c*602 – 64)

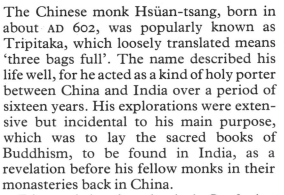

The Chinese monk Hsüan-tsang, born in about AD 602, was popularly known as Tripitaka, which loosely translated means 'three bags full'. The name described his life well, for he acted as a kind of holy porter between China and India over a period of sixteen years. His explorations were extensive but incidental to his main purpose, which was to lay the sacred books of Buddhism, to be found in India, as a revelation before his fellow monks in their monasteries back in China.

Educated in the classical Confucian tradition, which, with Taoism, was the central tradition of Chinese religion and thought, Hsüan-tsang was a convert to Buddhism, and an exceptional student. He therefore had a ready grasp of both Buddhist and Taoist texts and this, combined with his remarkable good looks, guaranteed that he would go far.

He determined early to travel to India to further his studies in Buddhist philosophy and applied for permission to leave the country. Although this was refused, he set out anyway, inspired by an opportune dream in which he tried to climb Mount Meru, slipped, fell and was carried by a heavenly wind to the summit.

Tripitaka's journeyings across the deserts of Central Asia and towering icy mountains of north-west India were subject to astonishing changes of fortune. Trying to sneak past the first Chinese frontier post, he was shot at with arrows and brought before the commander; this man, fortunately, was a sincere Buddhist and sent Tripitaka on his way with food and water. Tripitaka hired a guide and set out across the inhospitable wastes of the Gobi Desert, but before very long the guide defected and Tripitaka found himself alone, a prey to violent hallucinations – often experienced by desert travellers – in which armed horsemen thundered towards him, wheeling and clashing. A voice from heaven told him to keep calm; and the apparitions vanished. Nevertheless, he nearly died of thirst before he was found by a party of men from Turfan (in Sinkiang Province), who brought him to their ruler. The king swamped him with kindness and tried to persuade him to stay at his court and become his chief monk. Tripitaka refused and cajolery turned to threats. Tripitaka began a hunger strike and the king gave in, loaded him with gold, silver and rolls of cloth and provided him with a retinue of servants, horses and letters of introduction to other rulers along the route to India.

23

Thus equipped, the following spring the splendidly un-monkish caravan moved into the Pamirs via Kucha, crossing the Tien Shan range by following a dangerous route across a glacier on which his fellow travellers perished, then down to Issyk Kul and Tomak, on the road to Samarkand. When they ran into bandits, they grandly bought them off.

At Balkh, the city chosen by Alexander to be the scene of his marriage to Roxane, Tripitaka met a Buddhist monk with whom he travelled over the Hindu Kush towards Kapisi, where there was a monastery where he might find the sacred texts he was looking for. He was soon up to his ears in discussion of Buddhist propositions, particularly about the nature of reality. Was it or was it not an illusion? That anything existed as such, was clearly not worth a moment's consideration. The question was, did anything, however solid, flash into existence the moment it was seen and then disappear? Tripitaka excelled, we are informed, in philosophical enquiry, by reason of his grasp of his adversaries' point of view. They only knew how to put forward their own theories. He could dispute convincingly on any grounds he cared to choose.

His philosophical concerns in no way deterred him from explorations more typical of the tourist than the learned enquirer. Near Kapisi there was a famous cave where the shadow of the Buddha could reputedly be seen. The drawback was that the area had attracted brigands who preyed upon the visitors. Tripitaka encountered the brigands but somehow managed to persuade them to accompany him to the cave; and there they stood, bowing and chanting prayers in pitch darkness. As on other occasions, an other-worldly power came to Tripitaka's rescue. The shadow of the Buddha filled the cave: the terrified brigands took vows and the holy man went on his way to Peshawar and Srinagar, roaming through country conquered by Alexander the Great three centuries before. He crossed the Khyber Pass on his way to the Upper Indus, noting:

Perilous were the roads, and dark the gorges. Sometimes the pilgrim had to pass by loose cords, sometimes by light stretched iron chains. Here there were ledges hanging in mid-air; there flying bridges across abysses.

He was now on the threshold of the plains of India where he was to spend years wandering, studying, comparing and disputing. He travelled up and down the east and west coasts of India, visiting the sacred sites connected with the Buddha's life, collecting holy texts, statues of Buddha and relics. In one monastery he would find a hair from that holy head, in another a tooth, even a fingernail, besides objects in use during the master's lifetime, such as his stick and his begging bowl.

While journeying down the Ganges, Tripitaka's party was attacked by brigands who were after not only his goods but also his handsome person as a sacrifice to their goddess Durga. As he composed himself for death, in deep meditation and prayer, a sudden storm blew up, capsizing the brigands' boat. Terrified, the men begged forgiveness of Tripitaka, returned his property and set him free.

During the years he spent in the subcontinent the Chinese monk became a celebrated figure. He was accorded much honour and respect, even by the most powerful, and showered with gifts. When he decided to return to China it took him a long time to shake himself free of his various hosts.

At last he was on his way to Taxila and back to Kapisi, with an enormous baggage train, including a tame elephant. There were accidents and mishaps en route – as when some fifty of his precious texts fell into the river Indus as they were crossing it and he had to wait two months for more copies to be made. The elephant's enormous appetite threatened to overwhelm the porters' carrying capacity. In the end, near the foothills of the Pamir range, the

Left A contemporary sketch of Hsüan-tsang, known as the 'Great Traveller'.

Previous pages The giant Buddhas of Bamihan dominate the mountainous landscapes of Afghanistan today as they did in the seventh century when Hsüan-tsang described them.

Opposite Hsüan-tsang found himself a prey to strange fancies as he passed through the mountainous deserts, rocky outcrops and boulders which make up so much of the desolate landscape of Mongolia.

Above A glazed figure of a mounted drummer of the T'ang Dynasty gives an idea of the grandness of the retinue with which Tripitaka must have left Turfan for India.

massive beast stampeded at the sight of some brigands and, trumpeting defiance, hurled itself into a river. Perhaps breathing a prayer of thanks, Tripitaka proceeded via Kashgar, Khotan and Lop Nor towards Kwa-Chow.

In 645 he reached Chang-an, the capital of the T'ang empire, where his career of monkish exploration was given the accolade of a reception by the Emperor T'ai-tsung, who graciously forgave him for setting out without permission sixteen years before. He became a famous public figure, fêted wherever he went, so much so that he had to ask to be allowed to retreat to an out-of-the-way monastery. The emperor allotted him the Meditation Cloister at the Hung-Fu Monastery, but could not resist engaging him in conversation about the places and people he had visited and taking up much of the time which should have been devoted to writing and compiling. Indeed, the rest of his life was spent translating the 700-odd texts (altogether about eighty-four times the length of the Bible) he had brought back from India, and, under the emperor's orders, supervising the compilation of his *Memoirs of Western Countries*.

In 664 he suffered a bad fall from which he never recovered, though he was clear headed enough to demand the customary recitation of all the good deeds in his life. According to his biographer, Arthur Waley, after a period of silent meditation he was heard to murmur: 'Form is unreal. Perception, thought, action, knowledge – all unreal. The eye, the ear, the mind – all are unreal. Consciousness through the five senses is unreal. All the Twelve Causes, from ignorance to old age and death, are unreal. Enlightenment is unreal. Unreality itself is unreal.' This more or less sums up the thinking of the Buddhist Ideation Only School which Hsüan-tsang founded, and for which he is still honoured by Buddhists.

The Polos
(Marco Polo *c*1254–1324)

If it had not been for a writer called Rusticiano, who was in a Genoese prison with Marco Polo in 1298 after a battle between the galleys of Venice and Genoa, we would know very little today about the Polos, one of the greatest families of exploration the world has ever known. For it was Rusticiano who persuaded Marco to dictate to him an account of his prolonged travels to the court of the great Kublai Khan and beyond.

The Polos were minor noblemen of Venice. Niccolo and Maffeo, Marco's father and uncle, had been on a lucrative trading venture to the Crimea when, at Bokhara, they chanced to fall in with envoys to Kublai Khan and were persuaded to return with them to Cathay. The khan, feeling that the turn-the-other-cheek tenets of Christianity might work wonders on his uncouth Tartar hordes, asked the Polos to act as his ambassadors to the pope and to persuade the pope to send him a hundred Christian sages. However, when the Polos reached Acre they heard that Pope Clement VI had died, and it was to be some time before a successor was chosen. In the meantime they travelled on to Venice.

During his absence Niccolo's wife had died, and his son, Marco, whom he had never seen, was now fifteen years old. The boy was of an adventurous turn of mind, so the brothers took him with them back to Acre. Eventually Gregory X was elected pope, but he showed little interest in the Polos' project, allotting them only two Dominican friars, who turned back almost as soon as they had started out. That part of their mission a failure, the three decided to go to China by sea.

They crossed deserts infested with brigands to reach Hormuz in the Persian Gulf in 1272, but on seeing the sort of flimsy craft they were expected to travel in – 'The ships aren't even put together with iron nails, but sewn with twine!' – they decided not to risk the sea voyage but to go overland, riding through saline deserts to Balkh and the Pamir range, 15,600 feet above sea-level and 'said to be the highest place in the world'. After forty days in this cold waste they reached fertile Kashgar; they then headed south-east for 150 miles to Yarkand, where many of the inhabitants suffered from goitre. From Yarkand they followed the steps of Hsüan-tsang in the seventh century to Lop Nor, and then across the vast and inhospitable Gobi Desert, where young Marco described the hallucinatory phenomena of the desert – mirages and the eerie sounds of shifting

sands. Finally in 1275 they reached the court of Kublai Khan at Shangtu, after three and a half years on the road.

Shangtu was the 'Xanadu' of the nineteenth-century poet Coleridge. After reading Marco's excited description of its 'palace of marble and stone' and its 'walled space of no less than sixteen miles, with numerous springs and rivers and meadows', he was inspired to write the lines:

> In Xanadu did Kubla Khan
> A stately pleasure-dome decree:
> Where Alph, the sacred river, ran
> Through caverns measureless to man
> Down to a sunless sea.

The great khan took kindly to Marco, not only encouraging him to recount his impressions of foreign parts – he found official accounts immeasurably boring – but urging him to study Tartar languages. Marco was soon proficient in four, and thus equipped, was sent by his royal master to outlandish parts of the empire such as Yunnan, even as far as Tibet. He entered the huge civilian army of Chinese bureaucracy; he was created commissioner, second class, to the imperial council, and for a time he may even have become governor of

Opposite The embarkation of the Polos from Venice; an illumination from the fourteenth-century manuscript of *Les Livres du Graunt Caam.*

Below The birthday feast of the great khan, shown by the medieval European illuminator of *Les Livres du Graunt Caam* as a splendid European-style banquet.

the province of Yangchow.

All this was very profitable for the Polos. All three were still alive and all three prospered, although Marco's father and uncle did not reach such exalted positions.

After seventeen years all of them started thinking of returning to Venice. If they were growing older, so was the great khan. What if his successor were to be less kindly disposed towards foreigners? But the khan would not hear of their leaving: 'Why think of such a dangerous journey? If it is riches you want, I will double what you have already.' However, an opportunity to leave soon presented itself.

Kublai's great nephew, Arghun, khan of Persia, had lost his favourite wife. With her dying breath she had asked for her replacement to be a Mongol princess of her own tribe. A candidate was duly selected to fill the role. But then the Persian khan's ambassadors got cold feet at the thought of travelling overland; local skirmishes made all such journeys hazardous. Seizing the opportunity, the Polos offered to escort the princess and the envoys to Persia by sea.

Their representations must have been skilful. The khan reluctantly gave in, making the best of it by extracting a promise that they would return after delivering friendly messages to all the kings of Christendom. Having agreed to let them go, he determined to send them off in style,

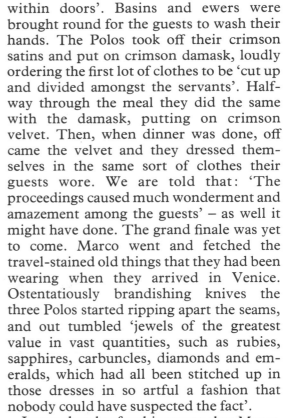

in fourteen five-masted ships. Thus, in 1292, the three merchant adventurers were homeward bound.

In those days a voyage was not only hazardous but timeless. Detained in Sumatra by monsoons, they took over two years to crawl through the Straits of Malacca, round the coast of Ceylon and on to Persia. Two out of three of the Persian special envoys died, presumably from scurvy or cholera, or by drowning, and so did a good many of the seamen. But the Polos survived the voyage and so did their charge, the princess, though her husband-designate had also died meanwhile, so she was allocated to his young son.

The Polos finally reached Venice in 1295, and, according to Giovanni Battista Ramusio, the sixteenth-century Italian geographer, their journey was crowned with an ending in pure comic-opera style. They found they had been away so long and had changed to much that nobody cared to come forward publicly and recognize them, so the Polos lost no time in putting on an elaborate charade.

Having established themselves within their own domestic circle at least, they sent out invitations to a grand party. Duly all the guests assembled. There was no sign of their hosts until they sat down to dinner, when a door opened and in marched the Polos, '. . . all three clothed in crimson satin, fashioned in long robes reaching to the ground, such as people in those days wore within doors'. Basins and ewers were brought round for the guests to wash their hands. The Polos took off their crimson satins and put on crimson damask, loudly ordering the first lot of clothes to be 'cut up and divided amongst the servants'. Half-way through the meal they did the same with the damask, putting on crimson velvet. Then, when dinner was done, off came the velvet and they dressed themselves in the same sort of clothes their guests wore. We are told that: 'The proceedings caused much wonderment and amazement among the guests' – as well it might have done. The grand finale was yet to come. Marco went and fetched the travel-stained old things that they had been wearing when they arrived in Venice. Ostentatiously brandishing knives the three Polos started ripping apart the seams, and out tumbled 'jewels of the greatest value in vast quantities, such as rubies, sapphires, carbuncles, diamonds and emeralds, which had all been stitched up in those dresses in so artful a fashion that nobody could have suspected the fact'.

It was shortly after his return that Marco was taken prisoner by the Genoese and encountered Rusticiano. His book, *The Travels of Marco Polo*, was an immediate success. Medieval Europe was eager to learn about the mysterious East, its fabled riches and strange customs. Marco brought them tales of China in all its vastness and splendour. He told them of the great cities and palaces – of Kinsai (Hangchow), the 'Venice of the East', with its twelve thousand bridges; of Khan-balek (Peking), with its twenty-four miles of city walls and eight palaces. In one of these, the Lord's Great Palace, the walls were covered with gold and silver and there was a banqueting hall large enough to seat 6000 people. He wrote of the immense population, their farming and manufacturing techniques, the ways of government and the vast bureaucracy it employed; of the great rivers, the advanced canal system and the huge fleet of ocean-going junks.

So fantastic was his account that he was accused of exaggeration. Yet as he lay on his deathbed in 1324, he protested: 'I have not told one half of what I saw!'

Ibn Battūta
(1304 – 78)

A Berber born in Tangier in 1304, the son of a judge, Ibn Battūta was a near-contemporary of Marco Polo who spent most of his life travelling. As he was not a trader, what can have impelled him to embark upon such a career, in those days so dangerous? Apparently the desire to become a *hadji* (to make the pilgrimage to Mecca demanded of every adult Muslim) was the mainspring. But his natural curiosity and taste for adventure led him to explore for the rest of his days – not for reasons of trade or religion but to see and learn about new people and places, satisfying his curiosity at the expense of his own ingenuity and other people's money. A young man's ideal, as old as the hills, but Ibn Battūta put it into practice, travelling further even than the Polos; and by recording what happened to him on his journeys he assured his lasting fame.

Curiously, in spite of being so definitely one of the roaming kind, he was also very much of the marrying kind, procuring two wives for himself on the way to Mecca and another three in the Maldives. But domesticity sat lightly on him. In his memoirs he gives no details of connubial bliss.

In 1325, at the age of twenty-one, he set out for Mecca and arrived, via Tripoli and Misurata, in Alexandria. There he first recognized his insatiable passion for travel. He met an imam (the head of a Muslim community) who said: 'I perceive that you are fond of travelling.' Ibn Battūta writes: 'I said yes; although I had at that time no intention of travelling into very distant parts.' The imam replied: 'You must meet my brother in India, and my brother in Sindia, also my brother in China; and, when you see them, present my compliments to them.' 'I certainly will,' replied the young man; and claimed that later on he did so, though his journal does not actually mention the occasions.

He went on to visit the cave of Machpelah in Hebron where Abraham and Sarah were buried. Having visited Mecca and fulfilled his religious duty, he went on across the Arabian Desert to Isfahan and Shiraz, before returning to Mecca for a three-year stay. His studies qualified him for the title of 'theologian', which stood him in good stead when he renewed his travels to Aden and the Yemen. At Makdashu it was the custom for young men to come out from the city to greet the merchants off the ships and take them home with them. 'If there be a theologian or a noble on board, he takes up his residence with the kazi' wrote Battūta. 'When it was heard that I was there, the kazi came with his students to the beach: and I took up my abode with him.' He was then introduced to the sultan.

Over and over again in his wanderings, Battūta seems to have fallen on his feet. This might have been because of his theological expertise; but it somehow seems more likely that he was a really marvellous guest, prepared to sing for his supper. The traditional obligations of hospitality throughout the Muslim world gave an opening, of which both host and guest were eager to take advantage. For instance, in Birki, beyond Arzerrum: 'The king . . . sent fruit and food to us during the time we remained there; and, when I had bidden him farewell, he sent me a thousand *dirhems*, with one hundred *mithkals* of gold,

Opposite The shore of Sri Lanka (Ceylon) visited by Ibn Battūta as he hastily resumed his travels after quarrelling with the vizier of the Maldive Islands.

Below The monk Baline greets the young Mohammed: a delightful illumination from Rashid-al-Din's *World History*, showing the most practical form of transport in the desert: the camel.

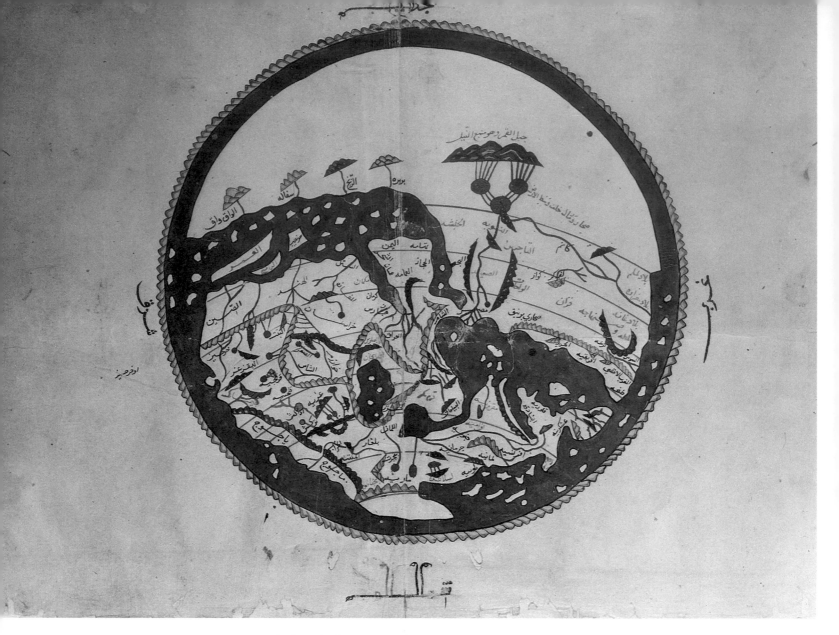

Above At the beginning of a manuscript of 1533 appears the Al-Idrisi world map, showing the Arab view of the earth's geography. It is not easy to follow, being to us 'upside down'.

and also clothing, two horses and a slave.' And Muhammed Ozbeg (khan of the Golden Horde, 'one of the seven great kings of the world') 'received me very graciously, and afterwards sent me some sheep and a horse, with a leather bag of *kimiz*, which is the milk of a mare; and very much valued among them as a beverage.' He even managed to persuade the khan (who, at first, 'refused, on account of some fears which he entertained respecting me') to allow him to travel to Constantinople with one of the khan's wives – *and* to give him 'fifteen hundred *dinars*, a dress of honour, and several horses'.

So, well provided for by his hosts, Ibn Battūta travelled ever onwards. He reached Balkh (which had been completely destroyed by Genghis Khan), and then at last India. Here he did extraordinarily well. 'I have no desire either for rule or writership,' he declared in doing homage to the emperor, 'but in our family we have always been judges and magistrates.' Whereupon the vizier said: 'The Lord of the World appoints you to the office of judge in Delhi.'

With the appointment went 12,000 *dinars* a year and some rents from village lands; yet it didn't take him long to get into debt to the tune of 55,000 *dinars*. So he composed a hymn of praise to his master, in Arabic, and read it aloud to him. The emperor was delighted. Striking while the iron was hot, Ibn Battūta mentioned his debt and the emperor ordered it to be paid with money from his own treasury.

Battūta fell from favour when the emperor took against him for visiting the cave of a sheikh who had incurred his displeasure. Others in a similar position were condemned to death, but Battūta not only managed to get off but also to secure an appointment as the emperor's ambassador to China.

Suitably equipped with dresses of honour, horses and money, Ibn Battūta was on his way again. Hardly had he set out before he was attacked and robbed: he passed seven anxious days, 'during which I experienced the greatest horrors', his food being the fruit and leaves of mountain trees; but the emperor reimbursed him.

Near Calicut on the Malabar coast, he lost his baggage again in a shipwreck and was left with only 'my prostration carpet and ten *dinars* which had been given me by some holy men'. Recovering, with his usual aplomb he was soon visiting the Maldive Islands, where the vizier made him a judge and gave him not only female slaves but three wives to marry. By one he had a son, the other two he divorced. Even so, he could not settle down; it was not long before he quarrelled with the vizier and had to leave hurriedly for Ceylon.

Very soon he was on the move again, travelling in a Chinese junk from Bengal to Sumatra and then heading for Zartou in China. Shipwrecked once more, Battūta finally reached China, and travelled inland to Peking. His account of his travels in China is brief and of doubtful veracity, but it seems that he continued to meet strange people. A cave-dwelling saint ('upwards of two hundred years old') seized his hand and smelt it, declaring to his interpreter: 'This man is just as much attached to this world, as we are to the next!' – a verdict with which Battūta could hardly argue.

In spite of his shrewdness, he was capable of making some extraordinary errors. He accurately described the process of pearl fishing off Bahrain, but then went on to add: '. . . the shells opened, they find in each a piece of flesh, which being cut away with a knife and exposed to the air, hardens and becomes a pearl.' It casts doubt on another observation about a part of Java called Tawalisi, where he said he encountered a queen with 'a regiment of women, who fight with her like men'.

At length, after twenty-four years of travelling, he arrived back in Tangier in 1349, having made one last visit to Mecca on the way. But he soon set off again, first to Granada in Spain, then to western Sudan; on his last journey he crossed the Sahara to visit Timbuktu and Mali. And there, as usual, it was not long before he heard the magic words, 'the sultan has sent you a present'. 'I hesitated,' said the old adventurer, 'expecting that a dress of honour, some horses, and other valuables, had been sent. But behold! There were only three crusts of bread, a piece of fried fish, and a dish of sour milk. I smiled at their simplicity . . . .'

We must be thankful that the sultan of Morocco ordered his secretary to take down a detailed account of the many journeys. Ibn Battūta had visited nearly every Muslim country and met many of their rulers. The book is a valuable account of the political, social and cultural life of the Muslim world in the fourteenth century, written with a particularly human approach. It ends with the comment:

No person of sense can fail to see that this sheikh is the traveller of our age; and he who should call him the traveller of the whole body of Islam would not exceed the truth.

Left A painting contemporary with Ibn Battūta showing two nomad travellers in conversation. Bandits kept desert travellers in fear of their lives.

Below Pearl fishing was deliberately kept a mystery by the merchants of Bahrain. Ibn Battūta could be pardoned for thinking that: 'the shells opened, they find in each a piece of flesh, which being cut away with a knife and exposed to air, hardens and becomes a pearl'. (Off the Malabar coast, from *Les Livres du Graunt Caam*.)

Henri Mouhot
(1826 – 61)

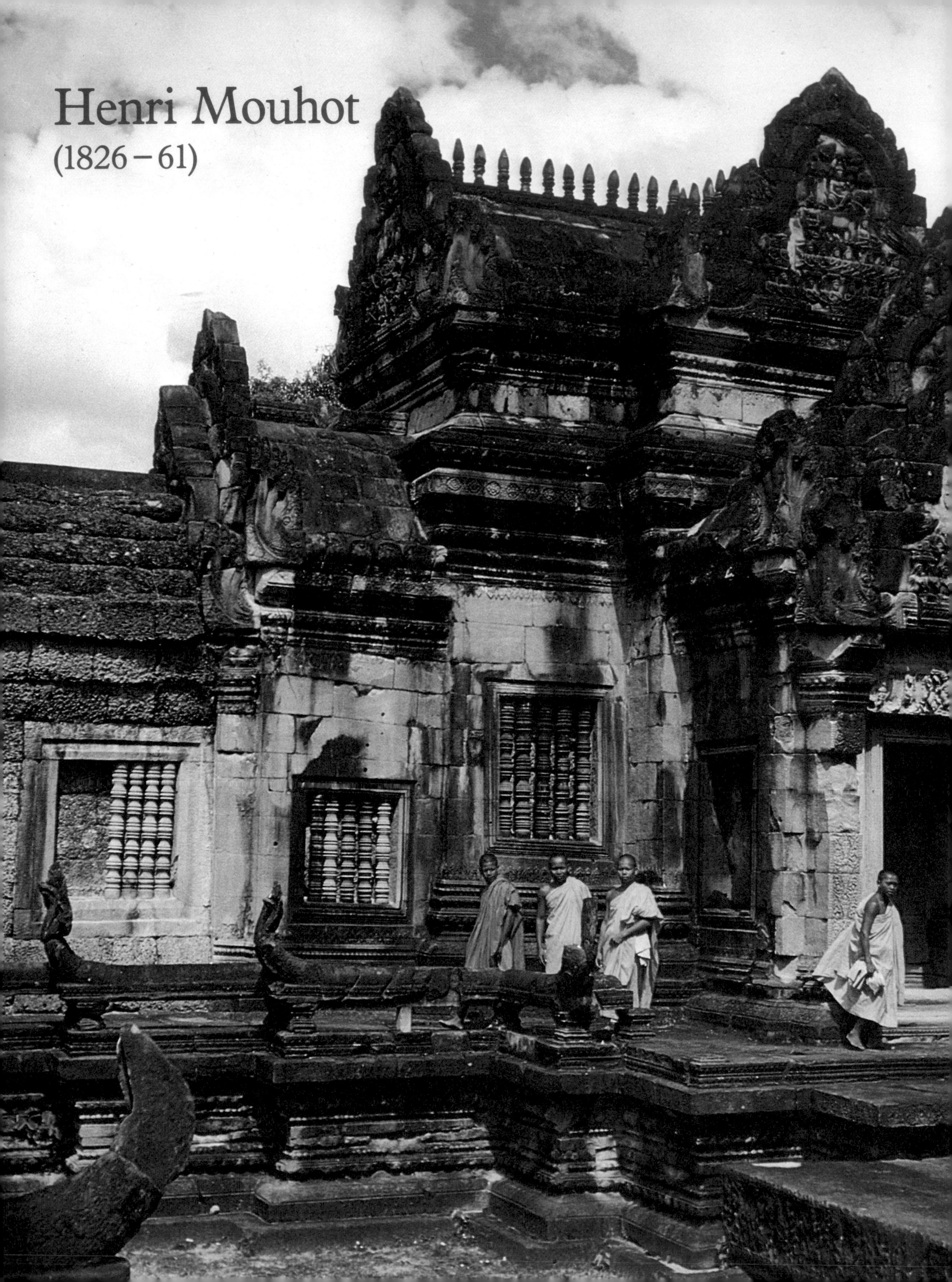

An innocent at large in the 1850s, the Frenchman Henri Mouhot roamed the jungles of the Mekong River basin, collecting new species of mammals, reptiles and fishes in Siam, Laos and Cambodia. So remote was this area that Mouhot stumbled across the remains of a civilization which, even five centuries after Ibn Baṭṭūta, remained undiscovered.

His father had occupied a subordinate post in the administration under Louis-Philippe and the republic, 'and expended nearly the whole of his salary in the education of his two sons'. Henri became an academic and studied philology in Russia. He was soon caught up in the wave of enthusiasm for the new art of photography which followed the exploitation of Louis Daguerre's invention, and he and his brother travelled round the Continent making daguerreotypes of works of art and famous landscapes. They both married Englishwomen (descendants of the Scots explorer of Africa, Mungo Park) and moved to England in 1856. Mouhot then set up house in Jersey 'devoting himself particularly to ornithology and conchology [the study of birds and shells]'.

It so happened that a book on Siam came into his possession, 'as though sent by the hand of destiny'. Fired by scientific curiosity and enthusiasm, Mouhot approached the Royal Geographical Society and the Royal Zoological Society with a scheme for an expedition to Siam, found encouragement from both quarters, and in April 1858 embarked in a sailing ship of very modest pretensions for Singapore. 'I spare the reader the details of the voyage and of my life aboard ship,' said Mouhot, disappointingly, 'and shall merely state that there were annoyances in plenty, both as regards the accommodation for the passengers and the conduct of the captain, whose sobriety was more than doubtful.'

Mouhot was severe on the captain, himself believing in 'abstinence, all but total, from wine and spirits'. 'I am sober, and drink nothing but tea,' he wrote to his brother, from Bangkok. 'My food is the same as that of the natives, dried fish and rice, and sometimes a little game which I shoot, and roast on a spit after the fashion of the natives, that is, by two bamboos stuck into the ground and another laid horizontally on them. . . .'

Starting at the top, he interviewed the king of Siam, who gave him 'a little bag of green silk, containing some of the gold and silver coins of the country', a courtesy which took him by surprise. He observed

Above Henri Mouhot, himself an expert in the taking of daguerreotypes, drawn by M. H. Rousseau from a photograph.

Opposite Buddhist monks in saffron robes still make use of the little temple of Banteay Sreay, Angkor.

that Siam was called by its natives *Thai*, meaning 'free', and that the modern name of Siam was developed from *sajam*, 'the brown race'.

His plunge into the jungle started in October 1858, when he paddled up the Menam River. 'It took us five days to go about seventy miles,' he wrote, in wonder. 'We suffered dreadfully from the mosquitoes . . . they were so numerous that you could catch them by the handful, and their hum resembles that of a hive of bees.'

He returned to Bangkok and then set out for Cambodia in December, where once again his first priority was to meet the king. He achieved this in peculiar circumstances. The train of escorting boats was headed by a famous pirate called Mun Suy, brandishing a halberd surmounted by a crescent. This fat little character was, as it were, a robber under royal licence who had been allowed to hide out in the palace.

The king entertained Mouhot to tea, offered him a cigar and wound up a music box which played French patriotic songs. Then Mouhot retreated to the only lodging for strangers there was in Komput, where he found that a former French ambassador's sailors had scratched some typically wry observations on the walls: 'Good beds, sofas and dining tables – on the floor'; 'Sea-water bathing – in the river'.

Wherever he could, Mouhot stayed with missionaries who helped him and sometimes accompanied him on his archaeological rambles. Before he reached Phnom Penh, he visited a priest, a Monsieur Cordier, who warned him of the dangers he faced: 'The rains have begun and you are going to almost certain death, or will at least catch a fever, which will be followed by years of languor and suffering. Ask the Cambodians what they think of the forests . . . and propose to some of them to accompany you; you would not find one!' Indeed, as Mouhot already knew, in the rainy season the atmosphere was dreadfully damp and oppressive. 'In the thickest wood, where the sun scarcely penetrates, you might fancy yourself in a stove, and with the slightest exercise you are in a bath of perspiration,' he wrote. 'I trusted in God and went on my way.'

It was while he was pursuing his consuming interest in mammals, reptiles and fishes, in what he called the 'provinces of Battambang and Ongkor', that he stumbled – literally, because they were so intertwined in the roots of trees – across the massive ruins of Angkor Wat and Angkor Thom and other forgotten marvels of Khmer architecture. 'Grander than anything left to us by Greece or Rome,' wrote Mouhot excitedly, though he felt he had to add, 'and a sad contrast to the state of barbarism in which the nation is now plunged.' To his astonishment, the natives, when asked who had built Angkor Wat, gave one of four stock replies: 'It is the work of Par-Eun, the king of the angels'; or 'It is the work of the giants'; or 'It was built by the leprous king' (of whom there was both tradition and a statue, nearby); or when all else failed, 'It made itself!'

Of ruins, particularly of such vast and dramatic ruins as those of Angkor, words are less descriptive than pictures. Mouhot produced both and sent them to the *Tour du Monde* in Paris, and to the Royal Geographical Society in London, where they were acknowledged as one of the greatest archaeological discoveries of all time. They

Left This picture of monkeys forming a chain from an overhanging branch in order to tease a crocodile was drawn by Bocourt from a sketch by Mouhot, who delighted in all the sideshows of nature.

Below and opposite above Overwhelmed by the Cambodian jungle, the ruins of Angkor remained unknown, except to those who did not care, until Mouhot stumbled across them in the mid-nineteenth century.

were ruins of the Khmer civilization which had flourished from the ninth to the fourteenth century, when the inhabitants had been attacked and the reservoirs fell into disuse. From then on the jungle had ensnared and enmeshed, but not completely smothered, the magnificent buildings. Long, snake-like roots had probed and split asunder massive blocks of masonry, squeezing them to fragments; but much remained intact under the suffocating growth, though in places the hold of the jungle vegetation on the stones had grown too strong for easy separation. Mile after mile of sculptured wall, acre after acre of shrines and towers, steps and causeways and gigantic heads: and always the encroaching jungle, the heat, the insects, and at night, the flocks of twittering bats, covering the ground with tiny pellets of excrement. The whole was comparable only with the Mayan temple ruins of Yucatan, but on an even grander scale. It has dumbfounded every visitor ever since Mouhot first stumbled across it.

Mouhot died in 1861, not at Angkor, but on the way to Luong Prabang in Laos. In October he contracted the inevitable jungle

fever; he lasted until 10 November. Only three months before, he had written to his wife at home:

Do not be anxious when you think of your poor friend the traveller . . . . Truly I experience a degree of contentment, strength of soul and internal peace, which I have never known before.

Below Tree roots strangle and probe the ruins of Angkor Wat, the temple system built by Khmers who flourished between the ninth and fourteenth centuries.

Sven Hedin

(1865 – 1952)

In 1909 the Swedish explorer Sven Hedin, who had not only crossed and recrossed the 'Roof of the World' but, to an ever-increasing public of avid readers, seemed practically to have taken root there, was given a knighthood by Edward VII, via the British Minister in Stockholm. It was generally supposed that the recommendation had come from Lord Morley of Blackburn, Secretary of State for India, who had been single-handedly responsible for preventing Hedin from entering Tibet from India three years earlier. The two men shook hands 'in the presence of many hundreds of male and female geographers' at the Royal Geographical Society's dinner in Queen's Hall, London, and swore eternal friendship.

Hedin was born in Stockholm in 1865. In 1880, while still a boy, he saw the *Vega*, with Adolf Nordenskiöld aboard, steam into the harbour of his home town, having completed the North-east Passage: a sea route to the Far East, by way of the seas to the north of Asia, which had been sought by Europeans for centuries. 'From the quays, streets, windows and roofs, enthusiastic cheers roared like thunder,' recorded Hedin, 'and I thought, "I, too, would like to return home that way".' He thought he would like to be the first man to reach the North Pole, but the fancy did not last. At the age of twenty he was asked to go as a tutor to a young boy whose father worked for the Nobel brothers in Baku, on the Caspian Sea. It seemed to him a golden opportunity to journey to the threshold of Asia: 'Already in my imagination I heard the roar of the waves of the Caspian Sea and the clangour of caravan-bells .... I felt as if I possessed the key to the land of legend and adventure.'

For the next few years he travelled on horseback through Turkey and Persia, visiting Kut-el-Amara, Baghdad, Shiraz and Persepolis. By the time he reached Kermanshah, his circumstances were severely reduced and he had only his saddle and blanket to sell. There he called on Aga Mohammed Hussein, of whom he had heard in Bushire. He was greeted warmly: 'I walked the soft rugs in my dusty top-boots and worn garments, the only ones I possessed. He extended his hand and asked me to sit down ....' The next moment Hedin heard the words that the Muslim traveller Ibn Battūta must have heard so often: 'You must stay here as my guest. All I own is yours. You have but to command.'

In 1890 Hedin was appointed as an interpreter on a Swedish-Norwegian mis-

Above The explorer on a dromedary, in front of a Mongolian *yurt*.

Previous pages The desolate face of Mongolia in winter. Sven Hedin made 'a jolly journey, a wild and whizzing expedition on horseback, by sleigh and carriage through all of Central Asia'.

sion to the shah of Persia. When he left the ageing Shah Naser ed-Din, he set out to cross central Asia on a journey of 3600 miles, with three horses and a stable boy. He crossed the Kara Kum on horseback to Bokhara and Samarkand, where he wrote: 'On Christmas Eve I started on a jolly journey, a wild and whizzing expedition on horseback, by sleigh and carriage through all of central Asia.' And when he reached home in the spring of 1891 he wrote:

I felt like the conqueror of an immense territory; for I had traversed Caucasia, Mesopotamia, Persia, Russian Turkistan ... and had penetrated into Chinese Turkistan ... step by step I worked my way deeper towards the heart of the largest continent of the world. Now I was content with nothing less than to tread paths where no Europeans had ever set foot.

A journey which started in October 1893 was to take him across the 'Roof of the World' – at a cost of £2000 (about £40,000 today). This 'roof' was the high crumpled mountain mass on the borders of Russian Turkestan, Afghanistan, British Kashmir and Chinese Turkestan, where boundaries were theoretical lines on a map as yet undrawn in any detail. With Kirghiz tribesmen for servants, he left Tashkent in 1894 and crossed the Pamirs in mid-winter. Temperatures fell as low as $-38°$ Centigrade ($-35°$ Fahrenheit). They went over a pass more than 20,000 feet high and Hedin later wrote: 'I felt as if I were standing on the edge of the immeasurable space where worlds revolve for ever and ever. Only a step separated me from the stars'. Wandering in and out of China and Russia, from Karakul via the Sarik-Kol Valley, he eventually pitched his tent on the shores of Lake Yeshilkul. 'And from there I returned quietly and unnoticed to Russian territory.'

Leaving Kashgar in 1895, he crossed the Takla Makan Desert, thinking of Marco Polo, whose journey, like that of Hsüan-tsang before him, had taken him alongside the Gobi Desert to the east. The journey was agonizing: the desert was like a sea of sand with ridges like waves 150 feet high. After three days the party was short of water; in vain they dug ten feet into the sand to find fresh supplies, and struggled on through the dunes. When they were struck by a fifty-five mile an hour sand-storm, two days later, two camels had

already died. Four men and six camels now had one cup of water between them; five days later, two of the party were dead, having tried to quench their desperate thirst with camels' urine and sheep's blood. The next night only Hedin and one companion, Kasim, were still alive. They crawled on through the sand under the burning sun, and after another two days came upon a shattering find – their own footsteps. They had exhausted their strength going round in circles. The next day they came across the course of the Khotandaria. Kasim was now too weak to move, but Hedin crawled up the dry river bed: 'Suddenly I started and stopped short. A water-bird, a wild duck or goose, rose on whirring wings, and I heard a splash. The next moment I stood on the edge of a pool, seventy feet long and fifteen feet wide. . . . Then I drank and drank again.'

He continued his journey, uncovering ancient cities in the lands of the Takla Makan and the Lop Nor, with plaster buddhas and other relics. Admitting he was no archaeologist, he packed away what he could in his boxes: 'The scientific research I willingly left to the specialists.' In his three and a half year journey he had travelled a distance greater than that between the Poles and had mapped out 6500 miles.

Back in Europe he was fêted in Paris, St Petersburg, Berlin and London. The Royal Geographical Society gave him its founder's gold medal. He made friends with Stanley, the African explorer, and was invited to go and lecture in America, but refused to do so.

Another journey across the Tibetan plateau produced further acclaim. Resting after it for three years in Stockholm, he produced six volumes of writings and two volumes of maps. To Hedin's satisfaction, later travellers, such as Aurel Stein in 1908, used his rough maps and may have been saved by them.

In 1905 he set out yet again, to track down the source of the Brahmaputra, the Indus and Sutlej Rivers. He succeeded and added a new mountain range to the map: the Trans-Himalaya, which he crossed, in all, eight times. Others had previously surveyed parts of it; but as Lord Curzon, the British viceroy in India, said: 'It was reserved for Dr Hedin to . . . place it upon the map in its long, unbroken and massive significance.'

Hedin was not content to let his fame rest there: his life was to take a new twist. In

Above 'Negotiating the drift ice of the River Tarim at night.' In Hedin's book *Central Asia and Tibet* (1903) imaginative reconstructions took the place of the modern photograph.

Below A photograph from Hedin's book *Southern Tibet*, showing the expedition's yaks in the mountains south of Panggong-Tso.

Above 'The Caravan Marching through the Desert of Gobi' – accompanied by the caravan's faithful dog (from *Central Asia and Tibet*).

Below 'Tibetans of Transhimalaya': one of Hedin's photographs of the forbidding-looking people he encountered.

1912 he astounded his friends by issuing two booklets in which he accused Russia of designs upon Swedish and Norwegian northern territories. Then, carrying his newly developed anti-Russian fervour still further (and with a mixture of many other motives), he went off to Berlin shortly after the outbreak of the First World War, and there was treated as an honoured guest of the German army. Taking German war aims in his stride, he professed to 'understand' the violation of Belgian neutrality; then in 1916 he went further still, in seeming to excuse the Armenian atrocities.

The end of the war saw a return to happier fields. In 1927, at the age of sixty-two, Hedin again set out for the Gobi Desert on an expedition so thronged by Chinese students that it became known as 'the mobile university'. There was even an airship under the control of a meteorologist and a meteorological station was established on the banks of an unmapped river called the Edsingol.

During the Second World War Hedin displayed Fascist sympathies. He willingly travelled to Munich to receive an honorary doctorate. It was all the more strange, considering that, on his mother's side, he was a quarter Jewish; a fact the Nazi authorities were prepared to overlook, so keen were they to have him come as an ornament to their cause.

Sven Hedin could find his way across the Roof of the World but in the basements of political intrigue he was lost. Fortunately, his fame rests securely on adventure and exploration in Asia as a young courageous man of action, and not on his naïve support of the insupportable in his later years.

The New World

To the native Indians of North and South America the New World was anything but new; it was the only world. When, in the course of time, they were discovered by men from Europe it meant the destruction, either suddenly or gradually, of their civilizations.

The Viking Norsemen first saw the American continent in the ninth century and reached it in the eleventh. When they found that the land offered grapes for the plucking they attempted a kind of settlement, but were quickly discouraged, fought among themselves, fought the native 'Skraelings' (Indians), and disappeared back to Scandinavia.

In the fifteenth century, when trade became the chief reason for venturing into unknown areas, the New World was rediscovered, almost by accident, by Christopher Columbus, who was seeking a route westwards across the Atlantic to the rich lands of Asia. A map drawn by the Polos showed the Asian land mass extending much further east than it actually does, and when, in 1492, Columbus made landfall in the West Indies he was convinced that he had found an outpost of Cathay. In 1498 he reached the mainland of America, but he never realized that he had found the New World, and not the eastern extremity of the Old World.

Once discovered by one after another of the explorers, the New World was assaulted, wooed, robbed and converted to the 'true faith' by the newcomers. Hernan Cortes in Central America and Francisco Pizarro in South America penetrated to the heart of the centralized kingdoms of the Aztecs and Incas, hoodwinked the rulers and conquered the people, carrying away with them a great deal of gold in the process.

Other nations were quick to challenge Spanish supremacy. Elizabethan England produced a generation of courtiers, seamen, adventurers and merchants – romantic figures who were eager for voyages either of gain or discovery. Francis Drake was a licenced sea-pirate as well as the first Elizabethan to circumnavigate the globe; while Walter Raleigh went exploring in search of lands to colonize. Both were good servants of Queen Elizabeth, but whereas Drake's reward was a knighthood on board his own ship, Raleigh was imprisoned in the Tower of London and later executed.

On a continent penetrated but still not completely conquered, there was room for bold adventurous spirits. By the nineteenth century the North Americans had gained their independence from Britain and were beginning to penetrate into the uncharted interior of their continent. The spirit of the pioneers was exemplified by Lewis and Clark, whose exploration of the Mississippi delta helped to establish an American tradition of self-reliance in adversity.

As the interior of North America was being opened up so Europeans returned to the South American jungle, not to conquer it but to investigate and catalogue its abundant flora and fauna. We must turn to Alexander von Humboldt to find an example of intellectual exploration. He was one of the first of a new breed of academic geographers. Following his intrepid voyages on the river systems of the Orinoco and the Amazon, he attempted in his *Kosmos* to order the enormous amount of information he had collected into a geographical system embracing both the Old and New Worlds.

Explorers of North and South America

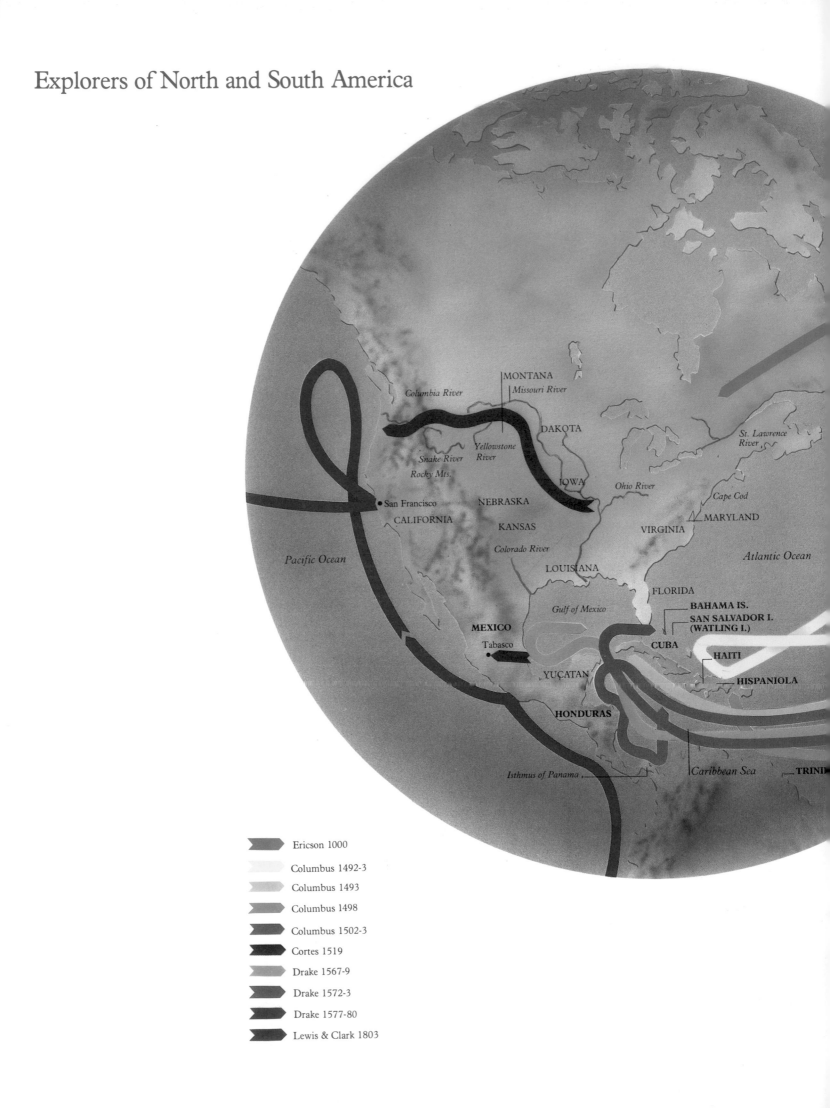

Columbia River
Missouri River
MONTANA
Yellowstone River
DAKOTA
Snake River
Rocky Mts.
IOWA
Ohio River
St. Lawrence River
San Francisco
NEBRASKA
Cape Cod
CALIFORNIA
MARYLAND
KANSAS
VIRGINIA
Colorado River
Atlantic Ocean
Pacific Ocean
LOUISIANA
FLORIDA
Gulf of Mexico
BAHAMA IS.
SAN SALVADOR I.
(WATLING I.)
MEXICO
CUBA
Tabasco
HAITI
YUCATAN
HISPANIOLA
HONDURAS
Isthmus of Panama
Caribbean Sea
TRINI

Ericson 1000
Columbus 1492-3
Columbus 1493
Columbus 1498
Columbus 1502-3
Cortes 1519
Drake 1567-9
Drake 1572-3
Drake 1577-80
Lewis & Clark 1803

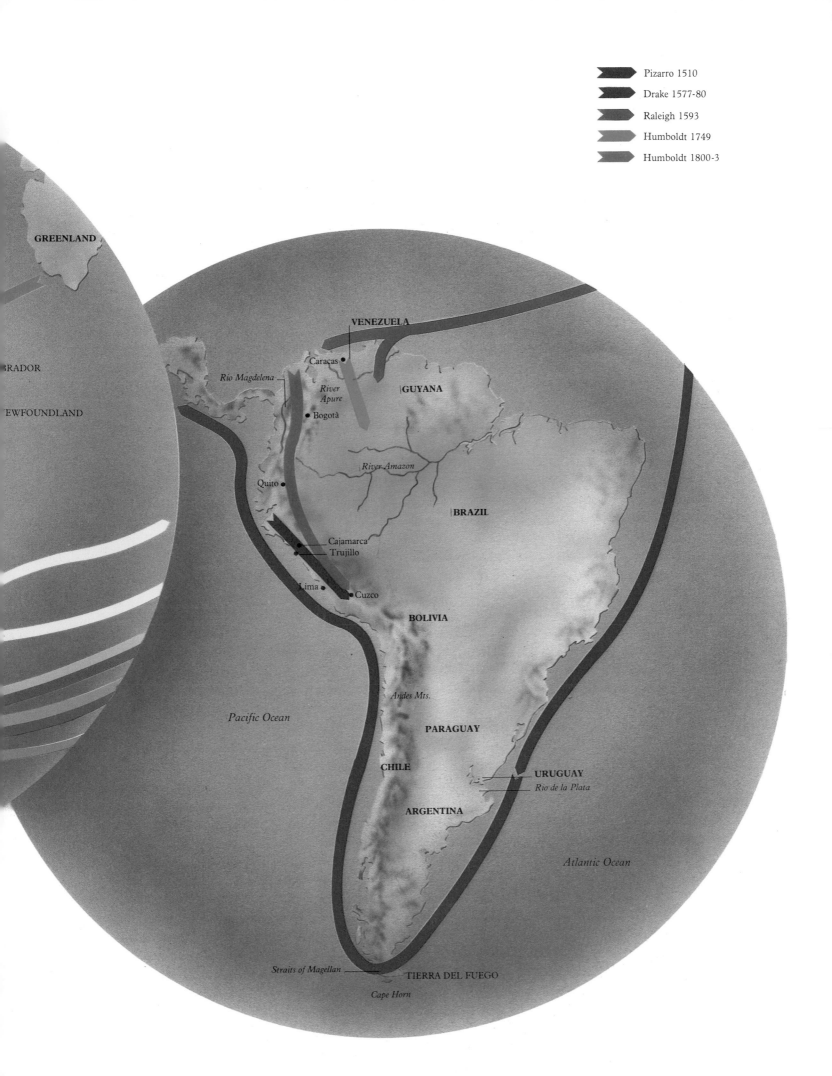

Pizarro 1510

Drake 1577-80

Raleigh 1593

Humboldt 1749

Humboldt 1800-3

GREENLAND

BRADOR

EWFOUNDLAND

VENEZUELA

Caracas

Rio Magdelena

River
Apure

GUYANA

Bogotà

River Amazon

Quito

BRAZIL

Cajamarca
Trujillo

Lima

Cuzco

BOLIVIA

Andes Mts.

Pacific Ocean

PARAGUAY

CHILE

URUGUAY

Rio de la Plata

ARGENTINA

Atlantic Ocean

Straits of Magellan

TIERRA DEL FUEGO

Cape Horn

Leif Ericson and his Family

(active *c*1000)

The Vikings, forced by the pressure of overpopulation to look for new lands away from the ragged craggy coasts of their native Scandinavia, took to the sea. To the south and east of them the prosperous shores of Europe were easy prey to their plundering ships. To the west of them lay the forbidding waters of the North Atlantic, and to embark on a course across these, like Eric the Red and his son Leif Ericson, required not only courage and toughness, but also superb seamanship and a desire to explore the unknown.

In 982 Eric the Red had discovered and colonized the west coast of Greenland (most of which is under two miles of ice, and anything but green). About ten years later the son of one of his followers was making the voyage from Greenland to Iceland when he was blown off-course far to the south-west. There he saw a land whose well-wooded slopes would provide much timber, which was scarce in Iceland. Hearing the tale, and prompted both by adventurous curiosity and by the Christian King Olaf of Norway's command that he should take Christianity to Greenland, the newly-converted Ericson set out from King Olaf's court in AD 1000 to find this new land. The thirty-six men of the expedition set sail in an ordinary Viking galley, a *knorr*, built of tarred and caulked pine planks, with a dragon-headed prow, a single coarse woollen sail, walrus-hide cables, and a bench where rowers sat side by side. With a good wind such a ship could make ten knots, but conditions on board were harsh, with the men crammed together with cattle, fodder and farming gear, and protected from the cold Atlantic winds and rain only by long woollen smocks and a small shelter up forward of the ship.

They navigated by the sun in daylight, and by the North Star at night, though both were often long invisible so far north, and calculated their speed by watching driftwood and bubbles. Thus it was, after many cold nights on the open ocean, that Ericson and his party made their first landfall at a desolate glaciated place covered in large flat stones, which Leif named *Helluland* ('Flatstone Land'), before coasting on southwards to find the sort of wooded country he had been led to expect, except that it was flat: 'The beach was low and covered with white sand in many places,' he reported, and called it *Markland* ('Forest Land'). There have been arguments as to the precise location of both countries, but it is likely that Ericson had landed on Labrador or Newfoundland.

From *The Greenlander's Saga* and *The Saga of Eric the Red*, passed on by word of mouth, and set down by fourteenth-century monks, much is known about Leif Ericson's landing in America, though the versions are conflicting. According to *The Greenlander's Saga*, they stood out to sea and scudded south before a north-east wind for two days until they sighted land again, an island to the north of the mainland. In fine weather they went ashore: 'They found dew on the grass, and touched it with their hands, and put it into their mouths, and it seemed to them that they had never tasted anything so sweet as this dew.' They went back on board and sailed into the channel between the island and the mainland, where the water was very shallow. The ship ran aground. At high tide they towed it up a river into a lake, cast anchor, took their leather bags ashore, 'and there built huts'. Ericson had finally made his most important landfall; and that is what has caused arguments ever since. Can it be proved that he reached Maryland or Virginia?

There they spent the winter, living in stone or turf huts and living off salmon from the river. They took note of the length of time between sunset and sunrise on the shortest day of the year and found night and day more equal than in Greenland (the

Opposite All that is left of the Viking settlement at Brattahlid. Eric the Red played a trick on his people by calling this country 'Greenland' when it was anything but green.

Below A Viking galley, shortened to fit on an eighth-century carved funerary stone.

actual measurements they made were proof that they were at least as far south as Newfoundland); and they rejoiced in the fact that they might not need barns for their animals' winter fodder because of the sprouting grass.

Then came a welcome surprise. One of the crew, a German called Tyrker, came back from a reconnaissance party so excited that he could speak only in his native language, and 'rolled his eyes in many directions and made wry faces'. When he had calmed down enough to make himself understood, he told them that he had found vines with grapes growing on them.

In the spring they left, laden with timber and grapes. Ericson called the land *Vinland*, which is as self-explanatory as the name 'Martha's Vineyard', south of the present-day Cape Cod, which many people like to think *is* the old site of Vinland.

In 1961 Helge Ingstad announced the discovery of eight Norse houses, together with a boat-house, cooking pits and a charcoal kiln, on the northern tip of Newfoundland. This find was probably more important than the 'Vinland map' published to the world in 1965. The Vinland map, it was claimed, had been drawn in 1440 – at least fifty years before Columbus went to America – but it immediately came under heavy fire, as a forgery. Its inks failed to produce a satisfactory time-scale answer when subjected to microscopic investigation; and at a Royal

Geographical Society symposium in 1974 the sceptical view prevailed decisively over the hopeful theory that it might be the earliest known map of Vinland. The symposium duly commented: 'The map's importance ... in relation to the Norse discovery of America was shown to have been grossly exaggerated. In this respect the publicity it had attracted had been particularly misleading.'

Leif Ericson could little have known what controversy his adventurous voyage would arouse far into the future. His brother, Thorvald, went back to Vinland the following year, spending the first winter in Leif's encampment. This time he met some 'Skraelings' (Indians) who from the shelter of a creek launched a war canoe at the intruders. The Skraelings were finally beaten off, but not before they had killed Thorvald, whose remains were interred nearby. A few years later, Ericson's other brother, Thorstein, made the voyage to Vinland to bring Thorvald's body home, but failed to find the new land, and died of plague on his return. Thorstein's widow, Gudrid, married again, a man called Thorfinn Karlsefni; she worked upon her second husband to mount a large expedition of four ships, 160 men, cattle and – to show they meant to found a settlement – some women. One of these was Freydis, Leif Ericson's sister, 'a very haughty woman', married to Thorvard, a man 'of no account'.

They settled down in Vinland with 'all

kinds of fish and good things'. The Skraelings duly appeared with furs and skins with which to barter for red cloth; they also wanted swords and spears, which Karlsefni would not allow.

A bull, which the Norsemen had brought with them, snorting and pawing the ground, terrified the Skraelings in the midst of their trade. They ran away, regrouped and returned to attack. It was Leif's sister Freydis who saved the day. She picked up a sword that had fallen from the hand of a dead Viking and, when the savages rushed her, 'drew out her breast from beneath her clothes and beat the sword upon it'. More terrified by her performance even than by the bull, the Skraelings vanished into the woods. All the same, guards had to be posted against a surprise attack. Finally Karlsefni, tired of losing men and of squabbles over the women amongst those remaining, sailed back to Greenland, leaving the dangerous new land to its native Indian inhabitants.

Next spring, Freydis and Thorvard tried their luck again, joining forces with two Norwegian brothers called Helge and Finnboge, who had their own ship. Being lucky enough to hit the exact spot of Leif Ericson's first settlement, Freydis laid claim to the huts as family property and turned the Norwegian brothers out to fend for themselves. Next, coveting their boat (which was larger than hers) she picked a quarrel, goaded her poor husband to avenge her fancied wrongs and, whilst the brothers were asleep, attacked and killed the whole party with the exception of five women. The pitiless Freydis then took the axe herself and killed the women, whom the men had refused to harm.

Swearing her party to secrecy, Freydis sailed with them, in one ship only, back to Greenland, with a story of having left the others behind to get on with things. Leif Ericson had now succeeded his father as ruler of Greenland, and dispensed justice to the survivors.

Whether Vinland was Newfoundland, Labrador, the mouth of the St Lawrence River, the coast of New England, or the eastern coast of the United States as far south as Florida, the geographical and historical evidence proves beyond doubt that the Norsemen's fierce courage and superb seamanship took them across the Atlantic from northern Europe to North America over a thousand years ago.

Below A Viking ship built in the year 850 was found at Oseberg and is now on special show at the Viking Ships Museum, Oslo. It was in *knorrs* like this that Ericson and his men navigated the Atlantic.

Christopher Columbus
(*c*1451 – 1506)

Throughout the night of 2 August 1492, the little church at Palos in southern Spain hummed with activity. Confessions in unusual numbers had already been heard. Mass succeeded mass until the early hours of the morning, attended by sailors in coarse canvas garments, their hair in ringlets or pigtails, together with their families and friends. This was nothing that the port was not accustomed to; except that the voyage for which the sailors were preparing promised to be both unusually mad and unusually exciting.

Cristóbal Colón had organized the venture, enlisting the aid of the Spanish rulers Ferdinand and Isabella. The town had scraped money together for the ships and some prominent citizens had even had to provide crews (the ruse of offering the jobs to convicted criminals having failed). At last, the *Santa Maria* (100 tons, 52 men, under Christopher Columbus), the *Pinta* (50 tons, 18 men, under Martin Pinzón), and the *Niña* (40 tons, 18 men, under Vincente Yanez, Pinzón's brother) weighed anchor. Three days later the *Pinta* lost her rudder, Columbus suspected sabotage, and they had to put in for repairs at Tenerife. Then at last the little convoy was on its way again, out into the unknown ocean in search of a route to the east.

Nearly ten years of preparation had preceded that glorious moment. Columbus was already about forty. The son of a weaver, he had been all his life the most enthusiastic of seamen and probably first went to sea at the age of fourteen. He had married well, into one of Portugal's first families, and had settled down in Madeira. He had exchanged letters with Paolo Toscanelli, a Florentine geographer, and between them, each encouraging the other, they conceived what to them seemed a rational plan for reaching Cathay – or at any rate, its outpost, Cipango (Japan) – by sailing west. Columbus knew the earth was a sphere, and relying on his reading of biblical sources, of Ptolemy's theory of the earth's circumference, and of Marco Polo's writings and maps, he reckoned that he had about 2570 miles of sailing. In fact, even if it were possible to sail westwards from Spain to Japan, the distance would be several times this; it was Marco Polo's overestimation of the breadth of Asia that caused Columbus' miscalculation. He also had a theory that the earth was pear-shaped, so the sea must gradually rise as he sailed westwards; and his ships, rising too, would the more nearly approach heaven.

Since the fall of Constantinople to the

Turks in 1453, the traditional route to the east and its rich resources of spices and silks had been cut. To outflank the Turks by sailing west to the Indies and so restart the lucrative trade was an impressive argument in favour of the scheme.

When Columbus first applied to King John of Portugal, he was referred to the Council for Geographical Affairs, which rejected the application out of hand. If there were to be exploration, they preferred the idea of sending ships to India around Africa. One ship was sent out, but after a few miles the sailors refused to continue on such a ludicrous voyage, and the ship returned to port. Disgusted, Columbus took himself off to Spain in 1484 and applied to Queen Isabella and King Ferdinand. From Cordova to Salamanca he persisted, his project being turned down by committee after committee. He applied to Portugal again, to France, even to Henry VII of England, all to no avail. At last, largely due to the influence of Isabella's treasurer, Santangel, the royal assent was won. Their Catholic Majesties became part and parcel of Columbus' venture, although he demanded an extraordinary price for his efforts: he and his heirs were to be admirals and viceroys of the Indies and all other lands he might discover, entitled to a tithe of everything 'found, bought or bartered within his jurisdiction'. People were soon saying that for a knave he was asking too much, and for a fool, not enough.

Had Columbus' sailors known they were in for a voyage of 12,000 rather than 2500 miles they might never have signed on, whatever the inducements. As they sailed westwards, there were near-mutinies on board when hopes that land was close by were dashed; and again when the compass, affected by unfamiliar magnetism, indicated that the Pole Star had apparently moved into an impossible position. A

Left Christopher Columbus: a portrait in the Uffizi Gallery, Florence.

Previous pages A General Chart of the Atlantic, produced in London by the cartographer Boazio in 1589.

Below The magnificent planisphere of Toscanelli, the Florentine geographer with whose help Columbus planned his journey westwards in search of Cathay (China) and Cipango (Japan). Its inaccuracies made Columbus doubt the evidence of his own eyes when he reached a new, instead of an old, world.

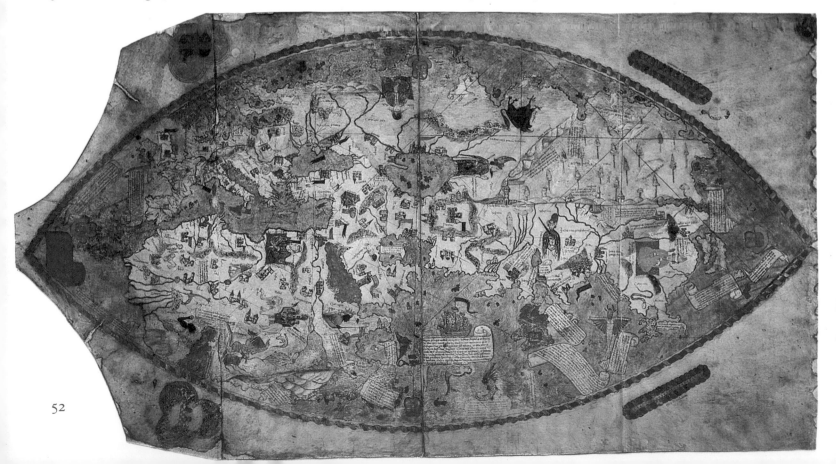

reward, a pension of ten thousand *maravedis*, was promised to the first man to see land. At last, at two in the morning on 12 October, after over two months at sea, land was sighted by a sailor on the *Pinta*.

It was Watling Island, in the Bahamas – Columbus christened it 'San Salvador'. He put on his finest clothes and, once ashore, went on his knees to give thanks to God. He took possession of the island in the name of Ferdinand and Isabella, then called for a vow of obedience to himself as their representative. The natives that appeared bowed and scraped gratifyingly before the strangers, with their unfamiliar pale skins and black beards. The Spaniards meanwhile were delighted to find that the islanders wore nose rings made of gold. They had found the three things sought by the Spanish and Portuguese explorers of the fifteenth and sixteenth centuries: land, gold and – for religious zeal was a strong motive force and was often used to justify oppression of native peoples – souls.

The tiny island, however, did not fit the European image of Japan, and Columbus' men, after discovering other islands in the Bahamas, set off to find the rich cities of Cipango (Japan), and the court of the Great Khan, which Marco Polo had described. On 28 October they reached the coast of Cuba, where the inhabitants were shy and friendly and spoke of gold in the interior; but Columbus sailed on to another island, which he named Española (Hispaniola), where there was evidence of cannibalism among the native Arawak Indians. Off Hispaniola the *Santa Maria* was wrecked on a reef and Columbus transferred to the *Niña*, and hastily set off to catch up with Martin Pinzón, who had made off on his own, hoping to be first home to Spain with news of the islands they had discovered.

On his way back to Spain, Columbus was blown off course by a storm and eventually landed in Portugal on 18 February 1493. Here, after his successful voyage, he was received by King John, who had refused to sponsor him ten years previously. Columbus went on to Palos and there was relieved to learn that he had arrived before Pinzón and so foiled any further attempts to take the credit. In fact Pinzón arrived soon after and died a few days later.

Columbus now set out for the court in splendid style; gold and jewellery, flowers and fruits, stuffed and live birds and finally, Indians themselves, enlivened his procession. Ferdinand and Isabella rose from their thrones to receive him, then knelt in prayer whilst the choir sang a heartfelt

Above A hanging: the implementation of Columbus' severe brand of justice.

Top The *Santa Maria*.

53

Right As 'Admiral of the Ocean Sea' Columbus had to tackle a certain amount of administration. At its least pleasant it could involve the hanging of his own countrymen. During his third voyage one of Columbus' sentences so enraged a Benedictine monk in Hispaniola that he excommunicated the 'Admiral' on the spot. Whereupon, in 1500, Columbus was sent back in irons to Spain.

Te Deum. For all the riches and honour showered upon him, Columbus still insisted that the reward of ten thousand *maravedis* to the first man to see land be paid to him, and not to the poor sailor who actually sighted it first.

In 1493 a second voyage, whose main object was the colonization of Hispaniola, saw seventeen ships with 1500 men aboard leaving Cadiz. During this cruise Columbus coasted along the shores of Cuba and made his men swear that it formed part of a continental mainland, which he still believed to be Asia. On his third voyage, in 1498, he really did see South America beyond Trinidad, and, mistaking it for an island, called it 'Isla Santa'. A great rush of fresh water from the Orinoco estuary at length convinced him that he was wrong. He concluded that the Orinoco was one of the four rivers of paradise, and that the pink-winged creatures dabbling at a distance in the bay must surely be angels, not flamingoes.

Meanwhile, things had gone badly for him in Spain. In Hispaniola and Haiti his colonial affairs had been running far from smoothly. Queen Isabella was horrified when she heard that the Indians, her new subjects, were being enslaved by the Spanish colonists. Columbus found himself superseded in Hispaniola, and was soon on his way back to Spain, a prisoner in irons. Popular indignation, however, prompted Isabella to restore him to her favour, and soon he was given permission for his fourth and last expedition, provided that he went nowhere near Hispaniola.

In 1502, again searching for a sea route to Asia, he reached the coast of Honduras where he met some Mayan Indians, inhabitants of Yucatan. They indicated that a rich land lay further west. But Columbus hardly listened. His head was full of fancies, and he imagined that the Isthmus of Panama was part of Malacca on the sealane to India. It was too late for him to change his views: 'I have reached the province of Mango which adjoins Cathay,' he declared.

On returning to Spain in 1504 he did not live long. He had not found a westward passage to Asia, but he was tenacious of his rights to the end: in a last codicil to his will, dated 19 May 1506, the day before he died, he demanded that the head of his house must never stop using the title of 'Admiral of the Ocean Sea'.

Hernan Cortes (1485–1547) and Francisco Pizarro (c1475–1541)

Above Hernan Cortes, conqueror of the Aztecs and 'gentle (meaning gentleman) corsair' as a young man, painted some time after his death.

Previous page Popocatepetl is one of the two volcanoes standing guard over Tenochtitlan, centre of the Aztec empire.

Like ferrets in a rabbit warren, the conquistadors (Spanish conquerors) quested through the tortuous highways and byways of the New World, mesmerizing their victims by their strength of purpose as much as by force of unfamiliar arms. Cortes, Pizarro and their fellow Spaniards had one thing in common – a sense of divine mission to save the souls of the heathen. That this conflicted with disgraceful behaviour towards their fellow men was a worry kept for the small hours of darkness. It scarcely influenced their daily programme of robbing, murdering and enslaving the South American Indians.

Hernan Cortes was thirty-three years old when he was chosen by the governor of Cuba to lead a colonizing expedition to Yucatan. A hearty, inspiring sort of man, ambitious and independent, who liked to call himself the 'gentle corsair' (gentleman pirate), he procured stores and men, not always paying for them, and in 1519 set sail with eleven ships, 500 soldiers and sixteen horses. His banner was a cross against a background of flames, his motto: 'Let us follow the cross and in that sign we will conquer!', and his declared aim was to reach the capital city of the Aztec empire that Juan de Grijalva had found in Mexico the previous year.

At Cozumel Island he was lucky to meet a fellow Spaniard, a priest called Aguilar, who, following a shipwreck, had been captured by the local natives, and then had escaped from the cage in which they were fattening him up for a cannibal feast. He was particularly valuable to Cortes, as he spoke Mayan, the tongue of his captors. After a skirmish at Tabasco, when the Yucatanis, who had never seen horses, mistook men on horseback for centaurs, he was much to the fore, helping celebrate Palm Sunday at an outdoor altar and interpreting the ceremony of bringing in the tribute – ornaments of gold together with twenty women.

Cortes quickly realized that the Aztecs would be a far more rewarding target than their vassals in Yucatan. The Aztec king, Moctezuma, had heard of the arrival of strange 'towers or small mountains floating on the waves of the sea'; as they could not write, the Aztecs had to make do with verbal reports of the thunder machines and the armour the invaders wore. It sounded as if the white-faced god-man Quetzalcoatl, long forecast in their legends, had finally reached their shores. It was safest to placate him with feather cloaks and ornaments of glittering gold. Moctezuma made the mistake of sending Cortes some all too splendid examples of the latter and at the same time demanding a tribute of human sacrifice from a province unwise enough to have welcomed the conquerors. To the Spaniards the message was clear: us or them, and 'they' had gold beyond the dreams of avarice.

Cortes hardly hesitated. Burning his boats to cut off all chance of retreat for his men and enlisting the sailors, a hundred of them, in his little army, he made for the heart of the Aztec empire, the city of Tenochtitlan. He force-marched his party over two high passes and through steamy forests, up to the central plateau. At Tlaxcala, one of the cities of the plateau region, he fought and beat the Tlaxcalans, who had no reason to feel loyalty towards their hated Aztec 'protectors' and joined forces with the Spaniards. The Aztecs' own unpopularity contributed to their undoing.

Tenochtitlan, at the time of Cortes' advance on it, was at the height of its splendour. Built on an island in the middle of a lake, 7500 feet above sea level, it was connected to the lake shore by three long causeways. Aquaducts supplied it with fresh water from the surrounding hills.

Riding high on a portable throne, a mass of feathers and gold, Moctezuma came out

to meet the Spaniards and conducted them into the city. In the palace the Spaniards saw gold and silver objects piled carelessly in heaps on the floor of a concealed room. Nearby was the temple of Huitzilopochtli, which had been dedicated in 1486 with the sacrifice of 70,000 victims. Priests with knives made of obsidian (so sharp that merely to touch the blade was to risk getting cut) slashed the hearts out of their living victims, laid them on the altar and hurled the still quivering bodies onto a pile at the bottom of the temple pyramid. Thousands and tens of thousands of them were sacrificed, more and more each day, in a desperate attempt to make up for the humiliations of defeat.

Seizing Moctezuma, Cortes used him as a hostage to subdue the people. Cortes' men behaved so disgracefully towards the

Aztecs that they rose in revolt, setting fire to the place in which Moctezuma was held prisoner. The Aztecs' own centralized government system did the rest, for it could go on functioning like an automaton, without a head. By the time that the Aztecs realized what was happening and chose another emperor, stoning Moctezuma as he pleaded with them to placate (or at least not further 'provoke') their conquerors, it was too late. As for Moctezuma, 'he tore off his bandages, would not eat, preserved an obstinate silence, with downcast eyes, from the time he was stoned by his own people until his death'. It was recorded that, to the astonishment of the Spanish soldiers, he even refused to kiss the crucifix as he died.

The Spaniards, quite out of control, were forced to withdraw to neighbouring Tlaxcala. It was on 13 August 1521 that

Above An eloquent picture of Spanish ill-treatment of native Americans: from de Bry's *Americae*, printed at the end of the sixteenth century.

Top Dwarfish and illiterate,
Francisco Pizarro, conqueror of the
Incas, was about fifty years old when
he started his career of exploration.
He was a plain spoken man, but
often jolly and generous.

Tenochtitlan finally fell, under amphibious attack, to Cortes. With the fall of Tenochtitlan (the site of modern Mexico City) the Aztec civilization, with its staggering sophistication, particularly in the field of engineering (with no metal tools, no wheel and no beasts of burden), was completely destroyed.

Yet few would mourn its passing, for in the Aztecs even the ruthless Spaniards had met a race more bloodthirsty than themselves.

As for Cortes, in 1592 he was given a marquisate and was received by Emperor Charles v at his court in Toledo. But his success gave rise to political jealousies and his enemies continually stirred up trouble for him. An expedition into southern California in 1536 showed that the explorer in him was still alive, but trouble went on accumulating for him in Spain; he returned home in 1540 and died in 1547, a disillusioned man.

South of Mexico and the city culture of the Aztecs lay the high Andes, the kingdom of the Incas, the next great American Indian civilization to fall. As the Aztec empire fell on the death of Moctezuma, so the Inca empire was doomed from the moment that its emperor, Atahualpa, was captured by Francisco Pizarro and his followers.

Francisco Pizarro's career followed an extraordinary parallel with that of Cortes, though on a somewhat less grand scale. Like Cortes, to whom he was vaguely related, he was born in the province of Estremadura, but he was quite another sort of man: a corsair certainly, but not a gentleman. Dwarfish and illiterate, he was plain in speech and character, but generous. He was also quite old – about fifty – when, with the similarly ageing Diego de Almagro, he set out in one ship with a hundred men to see what South America from Panama downwards might have to offer. A journey down the west coast revealed 300 miles of swamp, jungle and hostility. Almagro lost an eye; both nearly lost their lives. Yet all the time Pizarro was learning about the riches of the Inca people.

In 1528 he took himself off to Spain, with wares to tempt possible backers; things of gold and silver and vicuna skins, even a live llama. A year of peddling and pleading produced a welcome appointment from Charles v, that of governor and captain general of New Castille, a province stretching 600 miles down the newly discovered coast below Panama. Almagro was given a much smaller piece of land, and was jealous

Above The remains of the ancient Inca city of Vilcapampa at Machu Picchu. The temples made no use of the huge man-made pyramids common to Mayan and Aztec cultures.

Opposite In a desperate attempt to placate his Spanish conqueror, the emperor Moctezuma sent Cortes ornaments such as this pendant in the shape of a double-headed serpent, done in a mosaic of turquoise with nostrils in red shell and teeth in white shell. It was believed to have been worn originally by the high priest of Tlaloc, god of rain.

of his colleague from then on. With volunteers, including four of his half-brothers, Pizarro went back to Panama to consolidate; and consolidate he did, for Hernan Cortes sent him money and he managed to seize emeralds from one of the Peruvian towns (some of which his own men smashed to pieces, 'imagining that good emeralds, like diamonds, ought to bear the stroke of a hammer without breaking'). At last, in 1531, he set out to conquer Peru and the Incan empire. He had 180 men, thirty-seven horses, and their equipment; and that was all.

The unwieldy party performed the astonishing feat of picking a way up and over the treacherous peaks of the Andes mountains and making the gruelling descent of the eastern side. The emperor of the Incas, Atahualpa, used his efficient messenger system to order his villagers to feed and welcome the armed strangers as they toiled inland over the Andes. He considered that once completely cut off from reinforcements they could be rounded up whenever he wished. Atahualpa had already shown imperial ruthlessness by seizing his brother's pro-

vinces and slaughtering his followers in order to establish his own position. When Pizarro and the handful of men and horses that had survived the appalling journey arrived in Cajamarca, they found a splendid compound, flanked by a palace and a temple, the whole surrounded by a rampart of earth.

Pizarro sent his brother off to Atahualpa, who was only a league away, saying (whilst his ferret-like eyes darted hither and thither, checking the numbers and equipment of the Peruvian forces) that he had a message from the king of Spain to be delivered personally. Atahualpa took up the invitation and appeared next day, borne shoulder-high on a litter and surrounded by richly ornamented chiefs and an escort of four or five thousand soldiers.

He was greeted by a Spanish ecclesiastic, Valverde, holding a crucifix in one hand and a breviary in the other, who said that unless the emperor were immediately to embrace Christianity his people would be attacked by fire and sword. Through an inadequate interpreter, Atahualpa asked how he could become a Christian. 'By studying this book,' said

59

Above The ransom of a roomful of gold paid by the emperor Atahualpa to Pizarro later resulted in a wholesale melting down of golden objects. A toucan in gold and turquoise survived to bear witness to the taste and skill of Inca craftsmen.

Below The Trial and Death of Atahualpa, painted by an unknown artist of the Cuzco School.

Valverde, handing him a Bible. The emperor idly flicked the pages over: the unfamiliar writing meant nothing to him and he threw it on the ground. Thereupon Valverde screamed: 'To arms, Christians, to arms! The word of God is insulted!' As if at a prearranged signal, Pizarro's men instantly attacked, dragging the emperor by his hair from his litter and carrying him off in chains. The city was sacked and looted, and up to 10,000 Incas were massacred. Atahualpa offered to ransom himself for as much gold as would fill a large room in the palace and messengers were sent to all parts of Peru to amass it. It was estimated that the amount of gold brought

in was worth four million gold ducats, but it was all to no avail. Pizarro accused Atahualpa of plotting the destruction of the Spaniards, and in a travesty of a trial he was sentenced to be burned alive. As an act of clemency he was promised an easier death by garotting provided he would forswear his own gods and become a Christian. This he did. The evening after the trial he was duly baptized by Valverde; and, the next morning, strangled by Spanish soldiers.

Pizarro, eager for more booty and slaughter, set off with his remaining men on a road which the Incas had built 600 miles into the Peruvian Andes. In the mountains they sacked the city of Cuzco with its 200,000 inhabitants.

Thus by the end of 1533 the Incan empire, with all its skills (particularly architectural and engineering skills, which had built roads throughout the 2000 mile length of the empire), had vanished. Booty from Peru flooded all over Spanish possessions in the New World. Some made its way back to Spain, where it caused the reputation and honour of Pizarro to grow apace. He was made a marquis; and Almagro became marshal of Peru. But the two fell out, jealousy from years back coming to a head, and in Lima, in June 1541, Pizarro turned to face men sent to kill him by his one-time friend.

He fought with desperation, and his two pages and his brother died in his defence. Pizarro 'took three of his assailants to Hell with him' before he was stabbed in the throat. Reviling them to the last, he drew a cross with his own blood on the floor; and kissing it, expired. According to Bingley: 'His body was dragged into the church, when no one even dared to bury it, till a man, who had formerly been one of his servants, obtained permission to do so. This man was the sole mourner at his grave; and defrayed all the expenses of interment from his own funds.' So died a true conquistador who, like Cortes, with a tiny band of brothers had conquered an emperor and destroyed an empire.

Francis Drake (c1540–96) and Walter Raleigh (c1552–1618)

The distrait of ma

0   25   50   75   100   125   150   175   200

er sey on the south parts of the equinoctiall

The zyuer of plata

The cost of the brazil

cabo of St augustin

1591

Sir Francis Drake and Sir Walter Raleigh resembled each other – as well as their gingery royal mistress, Elizabeth of England – in that stories of their reputed doings took hold of the public imagination even more after their death than when they were alive. That Elizabeth herself was a virgin was no less improbable than that Drake, on 19 July 1588, was playing bowls after dinner on Plymouth Hoe when news came that the Spanish Armada had been sighted. 'We have time enough to finish the game and beat the Spaniards afterwards,' it was said that he said, wood in hand. As for Sir Walter: 'This Captain Raleigh coming out of Ireland to the English Court in good habit' (his clothes being then a considerable part of his estate) bowing low, with a grand sweep of his arm, spread out his cloak 'in a plashy place ... whereon the Queen trod gently over'. Apparently she rewarded him later 'with many suits for his so free and so seasonable tender of so fair a foot cloth'.

Drake was the eldest of twelve children of a Tavistock labourer turned Protestant lay preacher. He was brought up in Kent, and while still in his teens he became purser of a small vessel trading into Biscay; the ship was later left to him by her master when he died. Drake was fortunate enough to be related to the rich, seafaring Hawkins family of Plymouth and in 1567 sailed westwards with John Hawkins in the *Judith*. England in the second half of the sixteenth century had little direct income from either Asia or the New World; Portugal monopolized sea trade routes to the east, and the conquistadors had claimed the riches of Central and South America for Spain. England was not on friendly terms with Spain, and therefore had nothing to lose in plundering the Spanish bullion ships that regularly made the journey between the Old World and the New. Thus it was that Hawkins and Drake set out to intercept a Spanish fleet, loaded with gold and silver, sailing from Nombre de Dios, the Spanish bullion depot in Darien, to Spain. The encounter brought out aspects of the young Drake's character that were to dominate his life: distrust of the Catholic Spanish and a desire for their gold. For ten years he was a privateer (sea-pirate), commissioned by Elizabeth I, attacking Spaniards in the West Indies, and on the Spanish Main, and on one occasion attacking the treasury at Nombre de Dios.

With two ships and about 70 men, he actually succeeded in reaching the treasury, where a pile of silver bars (reputedly 70 feet in length, 10 in breadth, and 12 in height) astonished his men. Drake, however, had been badly wounded and was in no fit state to judge whether a commotion in the town boded counter-attack. He withdrew, disappointed, but thanking God; and then decided to attack a bullion convoy on land as it crossed the Isthmus of Panama. Taking no more than a handful of men he made friends with the native Cimarrones whom he used as guides. His attack was spoiled when one of his own men, the worse for drink, grabbed a passing man on horseback, thereby allowing a warning of ambush to be given. However, the Cimarrones showed Drake a tree with steps cut in it, from whose top he had a view of the Great South Sea. There – the story goes – he asked of God a blessing upon another project: the one with which history, above all else, has linked his name: the circumnavigation of the globe.

In 1577 his opportunity came. He was allowed to mount his expedition to the

South Sea, where a good deal of harm could be inflicted on the unguarded Spanish domains. The venture was backed by the queen, and before he sailed she granted him an audience during which she let it be known that she 'would gladly be revenged on the king of Spain for divers injuries'.

Drake's fleet consisted of five small ships, his own being the *Pelican*. With him he took 164 sailors and a mob of adventurers, goods of all sorts for barter and a small band of musicians. On board also was Thomas Doughty, a courtier, whom Drake had cause to try and execute in Patagonia for plotting against him, and Francis Fletcher, the chaplain, who kept a journal of the voyage, later published as *The World Encompassed*. According to Fletcher, after the trial Drake and Doughty knelt side by side to receive holy communion, dined together and then parted: Doughty to his execution, Drake to continue sailing round the world.

As Drake passed through the Straits of

Magellan, the prayer he had offered on first glimpsing the Pacific looked as if it would be granted. He had already abandoned two of his ships near the Rio de la Plata; two more missed a rendezvous and went back through the Straits to England. Drake in the *Pelican*, now renamed the *Golden Hind*, found himself alone in the Pacific, and blown south by a storm to the 'uttermost part of land towards the South Pole' where 'the Atlantic Ocean and the South Sea meet in a most large and free scope'.

Resetting his course, he headed up the coast of Chile, attacking Spanish ships whenever he could. Of these the *Nuestra Señora de la Concepción* (known to the sailors as *Cacafuego*) was his biggest prize. It took several days to transfer her cargo to the *Golden Hind*; its value, in gold and jewellery alone, ran to millions.

Near present-day San Francisco he was greeted by naked natives, who danced before him and gave him a crown of feathers. He called the place 'New Albion'

Above The *Armada Tapestry* in the National Maritime Museum, Greenwich, shows the Spanish Armada in full sail.

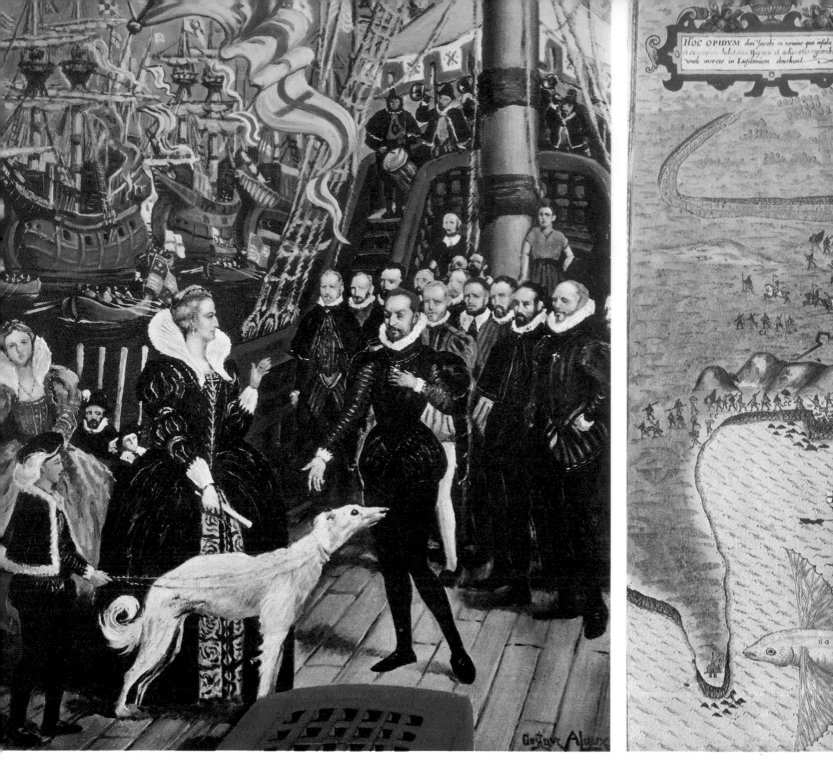

HOC OPIDVM *dui Jacobi co nomine quo infula*
et nauibus fuit cui fuper et aduentu eximiti
unde merces in Lufitaniam deuehunt

and left behind a monument, a post bearing
an engraved brass plate with a hole cut in it
to take an English sixpence.

Then for more than two months he sailed
across the Pacific. In October 1579 he
arrived in the Philippines and from there he
went on to Ternate in the Moluccas, when
his band of musicians came in useful: they
were sent in a boat to play to the sultan – to
create 'a musical paradise' – and to smooth
the way for discussions on an exclusive trade
agreement in spices for English merchants.
Then Drake was off again; the *Golden Hind*
ran aground on a rock off the Celebes but
was safely refloated and reached Java in
March 1580. In June he rounded the Cape
of Good Hope; and towards the end of
September Drake sailed into Plymouth,

enquiring of a startled fisherman whether
the queen were still alive. Indeed she was;
and she rewarded him with a knighthood on
board his own ship at Deptford.

Such things as 'singeing the King of
Spain's beard' (by attacking Spanish ships
in Cadiz harbour) and his famous encounter with the Spanish Armada were yet
to form part of Drake's career; but as
admiral, not explorer. Such exploits led on
to a final venture, nothing less than the
destruction of the little town of Nombre de
Dios, the scene of his former sortie against
the Spaniards. The town was no longer the
great terminal of the bullion fleet; the once
friendly Cimarrones had vanished. Drake
was suffering from dysentery: 'I never
thought a place could be so changed, as it

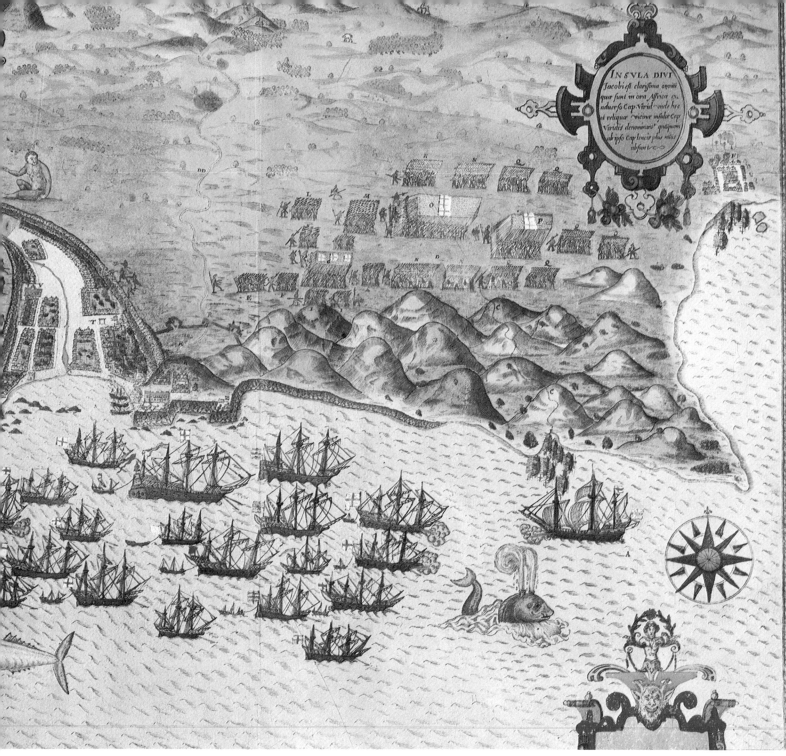

Above Drake's attack on Santiago gave rise to this picture, said to be the earliest view of any city now in the territories of the USA.

were from a delicious and pleasant arbour into a vast and desert wilderness' he said, in the manner of an old man visiting the scenes of his youth. Near Puerto Bello, on 28 January 1596, he weakened and died, aged only fifty.

He had sailed around the globe, as the Portuguese Magellan had done nearly sixty years before, and, like Magellan, he had made an important geographical discovery. Magellan had discovered the Straits named after him, which link the Atlantic and Pacific Oceans. Drake had discovered that this was not the only route; that south of Tierra del Fuego and Cape Horn was open and navigable sea. He had spent nearly three years 'in going through with so many adventures, in escaping out of so many dangers and overcoming so many difficulties in this our encompassing of this nether globe, and passing round the world'.

Sir Walter Raleigh, soldier, seaman, courtier, poet and explorer, was an equally dashing and romantic contemporary of Drake. According to the diarist John Aubrey, he had 'a most remarkable aspect, an exceeding high forehead, long-faced and sour eie-lidded, a kind of pigge-eie'. He wore his fortune on his person, 'a white sattin doublet, all embroidered with rich pearles' and chains and rings besides. But the handsome royal favourite had suddenly, after years of courtiership, followed the dictates of his heart, and was clapped in the Tower of London for seducing Elizabeth

Above Raleigh and his son. Raleigh was said to have scratched a message for Queen Elizabeth on a window pane: 'Fain would I climb, yet fear I to fall,' to which the Queen was supposed to have replied, by scratching: 'If thy heart fails thee, climb not at all.'

Throgmorton, one of Elizabeth's maids of honour. He was released from the Tower to help distribute loot from the Portuguese carrack, *Madre de Dios*, rich prize captured by the privateering expedition he was to have led before he was imprisoned.

Freed from the obligations of being a courtier, Raleigh devoted his energies to trying to establish a colony in Virginia between 1584 and 1589. He never went there himself and the colony failed. In 1595, however, he set off for Guyana, in South America, in search of adventure and the fabled civilization of El Dorado, the legendary 'country of the gilded man'. Leaving his ships off Trinidad, he ventured into the swamp and jungle country of the Orinoco River. The expedition found Indians and pineapples, but no golden treasure. Tall stories crept into Raleigh's account of the journey: they saw headless men with 'their eyes in their shoulders, and their mouths in the middle of their breasts', and Amazons 'who do accompanie with men but once in a yeere, and for the time of one moneth, which I gather by their relation to be in Aprill'.

In 1603 the queen died, and James I came to the throne. Raleigh had for a long time been a rival of the Earl of Essex, a favourite of James, and his strong anti-Spanish feeling made him yet more unpopular with the pacifist, Catholic king. He became implicated in the intrigues that surrounded the court in the early years of James' reign and was imprisoned in the Tower for plotting against the throne. There he spent thirteen years under sentence of death, writing, planning and reflecting. Sitting in his sombre cell he wrote this verse in his Bible:

> Even such is tyme, that takes in Trust
> Our Youth, our Joyes, our all we have,
> And payes us but with Earth and Dust.

A second Guyana expedition seemed to be his only way of escape. He promised to find a goldmine, one which, he guaranteed, would not be on Spanish land. James apparently supported him, yet gave the Spanish ambassador Gondomar a detailed summary of his plans, and promised to execute Raleigh on his return to England should he commit any act of piracy.

Raleigh's search for gold in the Orinoco was no more successful in 1618 than it had been in 1596. The only gold he found was in Spanish mines, and during the battle for one of these, at San Thomé, his son was mortally wounded.

On Raleigh's return, James used this incident as an excuse to implement his promise to Gondomar, and ordered the sentence of death passed previously to be carried out. Before going to the scaffold he smoked a pipe of tobacco – the weed he had brought back from Virginia to help demonstrate how fine a place for colonists that part of the New World would be. He had dreamed of turning North and South America into English colonies, but his achievement had not matched his imagination, daring and energy.

Meriwether Lewis (1774–1809) and William Clark (1770–1838)

Above Sacagawea, sister of the Shoshoni chief, with Lewis and Clark, on the Columbia River. Known as the 'Birdwoman' she was the third wife of the expedition's interpreter Charbonneau, by whom she had a child at the end of a long winter at Fort Mandan.

Previous page The Lewis and Clark expedition at the Great Falls of the Missouri by O. C. Seltzer.

'The object of your mission,' Thomas Jefferson instructed Meriwether Lewis,

is to explore the Missouri River, and such principal streams of it, as by its course and communication with the water of the Pacific Ocean, whether the Columbia, Oregon, Colorado, or any other river, may offer the most direct and practicable water-communication across the continent, for the purposes of commerce.

The year was 1803, the year of the Louisiana Purchase, when the United States obtained the vast, formerly French-owned territory stretching from the present-day state of Louisiana across the continent to the west and up as far as Montana. The Purchase more than doubled the existing territory of the United States, and cost fifteen million dollars.

For centuries Europeans had been exploring South, Central and North America. But now Captain Meriwether Lewis (Jefferson's private secretary) was to be sent into the new territory to find a route to the Pacific. Lewis picked Lieutenant William Clark as his deputy leader. From the start the expedition of some thirty men displayed an unusually democratic aspect.

Lewis and Clark were to be equal in rank and influence, and the arrangement worked throughout the expedition's hazardous progress through Indian territory.

On 14 May 1804 the party set out along the Missouri in three boats and two canoes, which meant that their average rate of progress was fifteen miles a day. The members of the party were required to be 'astronomers, ethnologists, geologists, engineers, physicians and surgeons, mineralogists, diplomatists and statesmen, naturalists, botanists, geographers, topographers and meteorologists'. All were unmarried, except their interpreter who had three wives; one of these was a Shoshoni Indian squaw, Sacagawea, who was invaluable to the party for her knowledge of Indian languages.

The expedition travelled 1600 miles through the prairies of Missouri, along the borders of Kansas, Nebraska and Iowa, and into Dakota. Near Omaha they smoked a peace pipe with the fierce Sioux Indians, and were allowed to cross their hunting grounds. One of the three sergeants in the party, Sergeant Floyd, kept a diary, which contained much apt description, along with some nice spelling: 'July 4th – We camped at one of the Butifules Praries I ever saw open and butifulley Divided with Hills and vallies all presenting themselves.' Alas, by August, Clark's diary (his spelling, too, was idiosyncratic) sadly reported: 'Sergeant Floyd is taken verry bad all at once with a biliose Chorlick we attempt to reliev him without success. ... Sgt Floyd much weaker. ... died with a great deal of composure, before his death he said to me "I am going away, I want you to write a letter." We buried him on the top of the bluff. ...'

On 8 October they reached Grand River, where they met the Aricara Indians. Clark noted that they made a great fuss of York, his servant, never having seen a black man before. 'Our men found no difficulty in procuring companions for the night,' he commented. 'The black man York participated largely in these favours; for, instead of inspiring any prejudice his colour seemed to procure him additional advantages from the Indians who desired to preserve among them some memorial of this wonderful stranger.'

They passed the first winter at Fort Mandan, a rough fortification they built which took its name from the local Indian tribe. There in February 1805 Sacagawea gave birth to a child. She was in labour when Captain Lewis was told by Monsieur Jessaume, a Frenchman living among the Indians, that he had 'frequently administered to persons in her situation a small dose of the rattle of rattlesnake'. Captain Lewis, who just happened to have a rattlesnake by

him at the precise moment, 'crumbled two of the rings of it between his fingers, and mixing it with a small quantity of water gave it to her'. Delivery took place within ten minutes!

In April the expedition left Fort Mandan, heading west, in six dugout canoes, towards what is now Montana. One of the more pleasant tasks along the way was the naming of hitherto unknown rivers: Maria's River was named after Lewis' cousin, Maria Wood, and the Judith River after the woman Clark would later marry. On they went, and in August they reached the Rockies. They loaded their baggage onto horses bought from the Indians and thus crossed the mountain ranges. When they reached the Clearwater River they built new canoes and set off down stream. They paddled down the

Above A Charles Russell painting of a typical buffalo hunt. Indians relied on buffalo for their main food supply. The animal has now been hunted almost to extinction.

Below A tranquil day in camp near the source of the Columbia River, an illustration by Henry Warre.

Above Study of a Grizzly by W. R. Leigh. Grizzly bears were only one of the many dangers encountered by Lewis and Clark.

Below The Robe Traders at Fort Benton by Charles Russell shows a Blackfoot Indian ready to bargain.

Clearwater to the Snake River, down the Snake to the Columbia River, and finally down the Columbia, negotiating many rapids, and into the Pacific.

It was in November when they reached the coast, built a fort and settled down for the winter. As before, the local Indian girls proved willing bedfellows: 'The females themselves solicit the favours of the other sex with the entire approbation of their friends. ... The person is in fact often the only property of a young female and it is therefore the medium of trade, the return for presents and the reward for services'.

On the way back to St Louis in March 1806, Clark split off from his companion to follow the Yellowstone River as far as the Missouri junction. Then he reunited with Lewis, who had been exploring his own Maria's River.

They reached St Louis in September 1806. They had travelled nearly 8000 miles in two and a half years, across totally unexplored country. Considering the perils the expedition encountered – hostile Indians, grizzly bears, rattlesnakes, sickness, near-starvation and exposure – it is extraordinary that only one man was lost during the two years they were away.

From their expedition resulted the first map of the Pacific route, and they noted fifty Indian tribes and over 200 botanical species. Seldom has any expedition in history so gripped the public imagination as this one, and the men who had taken part in it were held in high honour. One of them,

Patrick Gass, took to the bottle and then married at the age of sixty, when he made up for lost time by fathering seven children. When he was ninety he was converted to the Campbellite faith, which entailed being totally immersed in the Ohio River to the strains of 'Shall we gather at the river?'. Even after that, he survived another nine years. William Clark became governor of Missouri Territory in 1813, married twice, had seven children, and died at the age of sixty-eight as Superintendent of Indian Affairs.

Meriwether Lewis was made governor of Louisiana Territory in 1807, but his career took a bizarre and tragic turn. On his way to Washington, through Chickasaw country, he separated from his companions and rode on alone to the cabin of a Mrs Grinder, where he arrived, oddly attired in a loose white gown with blue stripes, and talking to himself. Bewildered by his strange movements and disjointed speech, she prepared a bed for him; but his servants, who had by then caught up with him, spread out bearskins and a buffalo robe on the floor, which was apparently what he preferred. During the night she heard him pacing about, talking to himself; then the report of a pistol, and something falling heavily to the floor, and the cry 'Oh Lord!' – then another shot. He begged the servants to finish him off with his rifle, saying, 'I am no coward; but I am *so* strong, *so hard to die*'. Two hours later he was dead.

Alexander von Humboldt

(1769 – 1859)

A European exploring South America three centuries after the conquistadors, Humboldt was motivated by very different interests from the desire for plunder, land and souls which drew his predecessors to the continent.

Born in Berlin in 1769, the son of a Prussian army major, Alexander von Humboldt turned to science at an early age, being known as 'the little apothecary'. His habit of mind, drily scientific for his work, was far from dull – his friend Arago, a firebrand in his time, said ruefully, 'He has the most malicious tongue of any man I know and the best heart.' Friendship meant much to him.

From the age of twenty, when he went on a scientific expedition up the Rhine, he knew he wanted to be an explorer. He was fascinated by the world around him, wanting to understand it better and explore its remoter regions. To this end he studied biology, geology, astronomy and languages. Early essays on mining and mineralogy and an increasing interest in magnetic forces showed the direction of Humboldt's talents. A meeting with George Forster, who had been with Captain Cook on his second voyage, had already turned his mind to foreign scientific exploration, but two of his plans were thwarted by restrictions on travel caused by the Napoleonic Wars. An expedition to Egypt, and another to South America and the Pacific fell through; but finally, thrown back on his own resources – luckily, he had a little money of his own – he planned with the French botanist Aimé Bonpland to visit and explore the Spanish colonies in Central and South America.

They left Corunna in 1799, in the *Pizarro*. His passport described him thus: 'Height, 5 ft 8 in. Hair, light brown. Eyes, grey. Nose, large. Mouth, rather large. Chin, well formed. Distinguishing marks, smallpox scars on open forehead.' What it could not add was that he was extremely good looking.

'I shall endeavour to find out how nature's forces act upon one another,' he wrote, 'and in what manner the geographic environment exerts its influence on animals and plants. In short, I must find out about the harmony in nature.' In February 1800 they set out from Caracas for the dusty river plains of Venezuela and the Orinoco. In the next five years they were to cover over 6000 miles on foot and horseback and in canoes, through some of the most inhospitable terrain in the world.

From Caracas they travelled south to

explore the Orinoco and its confluence with the Amazon and the Rio Negro. The humid heat of the dense tropical forests was stifling; insects and rain destroyed their provisions, and they were tormented by mosquitoes. They lived on ground-up cacao beans and river water when their food ran out, and of the Indians' eating habits reported: 'We hardly entered a hut without encountering the horrible remains of repasts on human flesh.' Yet the two scientists' excitement at the discoveries they were making ('we were barely able to collect a tenth of the specimens met with,'

wrote Humboldt) kept them healthy and energetic until they returned to Cuba three months later.

March was spent on the arid plains, in temperatures of up to 50° Centigrade (122° Fahrenheit). Here in the water-holes they encountered alligators and, to their astonishment, electric eels. They watched as the Indians drove terrified horses into the water (charged with up to 650 volts) to bring the eels to the surface. At the end of the month they reached the River Apuré, where they transferred their equipment to a canoe. Surrounded by fascinating and

unfamiliar animal life, they sailed down to the confluence with the Orinoco.

Here the landscape changed dramatically. At first the river was broad as a lake, with wide beaches frequented by turtles, but soon it narrowed, and the clear water became foully tainted by the putrefying remains of dead caymans on the banks. Then the river changed into a forty-mile-long series of perilous rapids, the Great Cataracts. Indians guided Humboldt and Bonpland through the rapids, to the brink of unknown, unexplored territory.

They were nearing the watershed be-

Above the well known painting by E. Ender of Humboldt and Bonpland in their jungle hut conveys an atmosphere of controlled disorder.

73

tween two vast river systems, the Orinoco and the Amazon basins, and at the beginning of May entered the Rio Negro, one of the most beautiful of the Amazon tributaries. The air and the water had cleared and freshened, and at one point, 1200 miles from the sea, they were surrounded by a school of freshwater dolphins. On 10 May Humboldt achieved his objective: the Orinoco forked, and a broad tributary, the Casiginare Canal, flowed off 180 miles to the south-west to join the Rio Negro. Thus he had proved that there was a navigable waterway connecting the two gigantic river systems of the Orinoco and the Amazon.

They took astronomic measurements to determine the point of connection, and then turned back carrying with them their 12,000 botanical specimens, ever aware of the power of the landscape surrounding them: 'Every object declares the grandeur of the power, the tenderness of Nature, from the boa constrictor, which can swallow a horse, down to the humming-bird, balancing itself on a chalice of a flower.'

After a short stay in Cuba, Humboldt and Bonpland returned to South America for another epic journey, this time in the Andes of Colombia, Ecuador and Peru. The first six weeks were spent on the Rio Magdalena, crossing 500 miles of uncharted jungle, before the 9000-foot ascent by mule train to Bogotà. On a series of steep, rocky and narrow paths they crossed the Andes from Colombia to Trujillo in Peru. In Quito province they climbed some of the highest peaks of the Andes, including Mount Chimborazo, which had never been climbed. Without the help of modern mountaineering equipment or oxygen, they reached 19,286 feet, suffering from nausea and giddiness, bloodshot eyes and bleeding lips and gums. Humboldt was the first man to attribute these symptoms of mountain sickness to lack of oxygen in the rarefied air at such altitudes, and in addition he calculated that the temperature, which he already knew fell one degree Fahrenheit for each degree of latitude travelling away from the equator, also dropped one degree for every 300 feet of altitude. This ascent, which brought him fame throughout the world, he counted as his greatest achievement.

The pair of scientists continued westwards, through the plains of the Upper Amazon, where 'an unknown world unfolds itself, rich in magnificent vegetation', to Trujillo, where they caught their first sight of the Pacific. The indefatigable

Humboldt busily set himself to study the climate of Peru and the currents of the Pacific Ocean, one of which was later named after him.

Their return to Europe in 1803 was delayed for a visit to the United States, where Humboldt was received by President Jefferson, who, following the Louisiana Purchase and the expedition of Lewis and Clark, had geographical affairs much on his mind. 'I have had the honour to see the first magistrate of this great republic living with the simplicity of a philosopher,' Humboldt said afterwards.

On his return, he settled in Paris to work on the immense amount of data and specimens he had collected on his journey. Until 1827 he stayed in Paris, the hub of the intellectual, artistic as well as the scientific world. He met and talked with scientists in every field, and gave encouragement and financial help to struggling students, even though he could sometimes ill afford it. He also appeared regularly in Parisian society and met the emperor. On meeting Humboldt, Napoleon is reputed to have said: 'I understand you collect plants, Monsieur?' 'Yes, I do.' 'So does my wife.' And without another word he moved on.

During those twenty years or so,

Humboldt poured out over thirty volumes of notes on his South American journey and much meteorological data. His *Personal Narrative of Travels to the Equinoctial Regions of America* is the first detailed and accurate account of the flora and fauna of the continent.

His return to Berlin merely enhanced his reputation. One of his projects was to further Gauss' experiments in magnetism; to that end he wrote to the Duke of Sussex to interest the British Government in expanding the European chain of observatories to include all parts of the British Empire. This was duly put into effect in 1839. He set to work on his gigantic *Kosmos*, with his young friends, as always, in and out of his modest lodgings. They were not the only interruptions. Frederick William III, king of Prussia, was his patron. When he died, his son became even more attached. Humboldt was soon in the position of Hsüan-tsang in the seventh century; his royal master swept him up and installed him in *Sans Souci*. Humboldt bore this stoically. He wrote: 'We passed the evening ... in a philosophical and literary solitude'. He also did a good deal of reading aloud to the king; and this (though he resented it taking up so much of his time)

he must have enjoyed. For when William IV suffered a mental collapse and his brother became Prince Regent, Humboldt was not at all pleased to find himself superseded by a young actor whose idea of a cultural evening was the latest novel. According to Kellner, 'Humboldt battled on and tried to break in as soon as his rival stopped to take a breath'. Defeated by younger and stronger lungs, the baron relapsed into gluttony on a large scale: 'He heaped his plate with foie gras, smoked eel, lobster, and other indigestibles and ate morosely.'

He died in 1859, in financial straits in spite of his patrons, owing money to Seifert, his servant. Three years before, a visitor, Bayard Taylor of the *New York Tribune*, remembered entering 'a plain, two storey house with a dull pink front' and being ushered by a 'stout square-faced man of about fifty' (Seifert) into 'a room filled with stuffed birds and objects of natural history, then into a large library' heaped with papers, books and documents. There he saw a man with abundant, snow-white hair, 'clear blue eyes, almost as bright

and steady as a child's' and a face with 'wrinkles few and small and his skin had a smoothness and delicacy rarely seen in old men'. Taylor noticed a chameleon in a glass case. Humboldt said drily: 'He can turn one eye towards heaven, while with the other he inspects the earth. There are many clergymen who have the same power.'

To the scandal of men of science everywhere, Humboldt left all his personal possessions to Seifert, who sold the famous library for a song to a Berlin firm. By later mischance, almost the entire collection went up in smoke at a fire at Sotheby's.

His final work, the gigantic *Kosmos*, was all but finished; though towards the end of his days his original clarity of purpose had been somewhat side-tracked. Nevertheless, in his life he had seen one thing and seen it clearly: 'Whether in the Amazonian forests or on the ridge of the high Andes I was ever aware that *one* breath, from pole to pole, breathes *one* single life into rocks, plants and animals and into the swelling breast of man.'

Australasia

When Prince Henry the Navigator of Portugal established a community of scholars dedicated to mapping and nautical instrument-making in the early fifteenth century, he was founding a power-house of energy for Portuguese explorers spreading their sails out into the uncharted world. Aside from rumours that some-where in Africa or the east there was a great Christian kingdom ruled by 'Prester John' the desire for trade with far-off lands meant reviving the idea of sending ships round the unknown southern cape of Africa to the east. After that the difficulties might be expected to diminish for, according to Chinese texts, a Roman ship had reached Tonkin in AD 166. Thus, after prolonged delay which only emphasized the extra-ordinary achievement of the ancients, in 1487 Bartholomew Diaz edged his way round Africa and into the Indian Ocean. The more extensive efforts of Vasco da Gama resulted directly in the founding of Portuguese influence in India and the East Indies.

Once some of the islands of the Indies were known and colonized, other nations could follow; in particular, Spain, Portugal's only rival in the fifteenth century; the English, towards the end of the sixteenth century; and later the French. Above all, from 1594 when Philip II closed the port of Lisbon to them, it was the Dutch traders who snatched at the Indonesian islands, as if at a lifeline in their battle against their former masters.

There were still some surprises in store; as when the theory of the great hypothetical continent of 'Terra Australis', a huge land mass in the southern latitudes required to 'balance' the land masses in the northern hemisphere, was finally proved false, and the more modest proportions of Australia and New Zealand discovered. Tasman's discovery of Van Diemen's Land (Tasmania) in 1642 led on to Cook's landing on the shores of Australia and Flinders' circumnavigation of the new continent. This put Australia (and even-tually New Zealand, also discovered by Tasman who thought it must be a coast of Terra Australis) into the English sphere.

The huge Australian land mass with its vast, dusty interior, presented a challenge which could not be refused. Many journeys were made across sections of it and many lives were lost in the deserts, where the Aborigines, from whom wise explorers learnt, managed to survive. The promise of emeralds and gold helped to promote a scramble into the parched expanses, and curiosity did the rest.

Meanwhile various European nations established suzerainty over the islands and mainlands of Australasia (Malaya, the Moluccas, Java, Sumatra, Guinea and others), drew up their own maps and made their own surveys. Thus by the middle of the nineteenth century the last of the five continents had been substantially mapped and the outline of the world map was largely complete.

Explorers of
Australasia

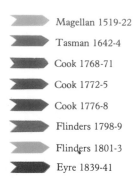
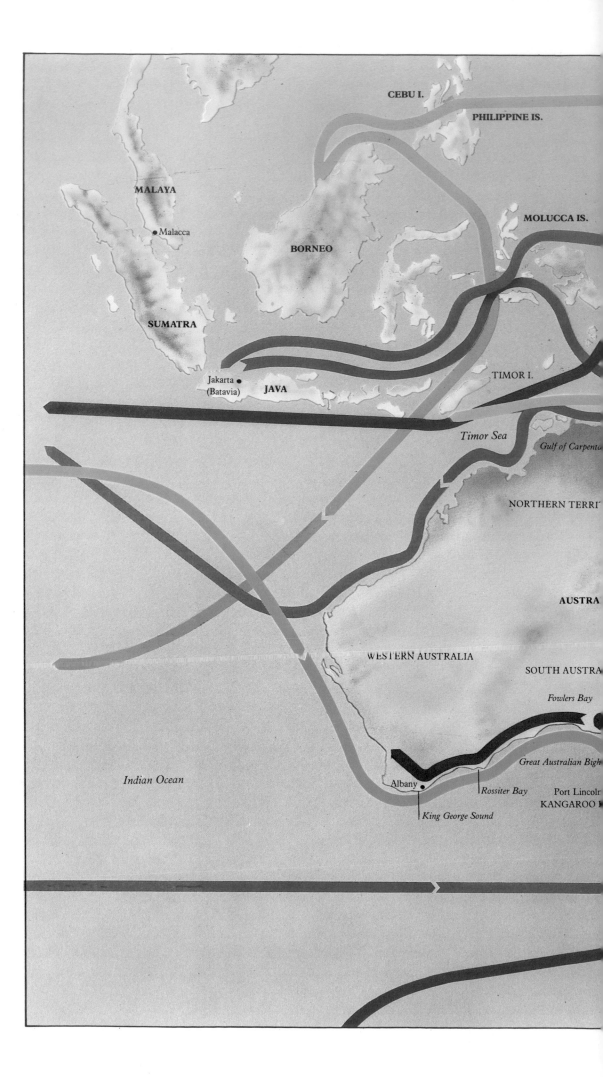

CEBU I.

PHILIPPINE IS.

MALAYA

• Malacca

BORNEO

MOLUCCA IS.

SUMATRA

Jakarta •
(Batavia)   JAVA

TIMOR I.

Timor Sea

Gulf of Carpenta

NORTHERN TERRI

AUSTRA

WESTERN AUSTRALIA

SOUTH AUSTRA

Fowlers Bay

Great Australian Bigh

Indian Ocean

Albany •

Rossiter Bay   Port Lincoln

KANGAROO

King George Sound

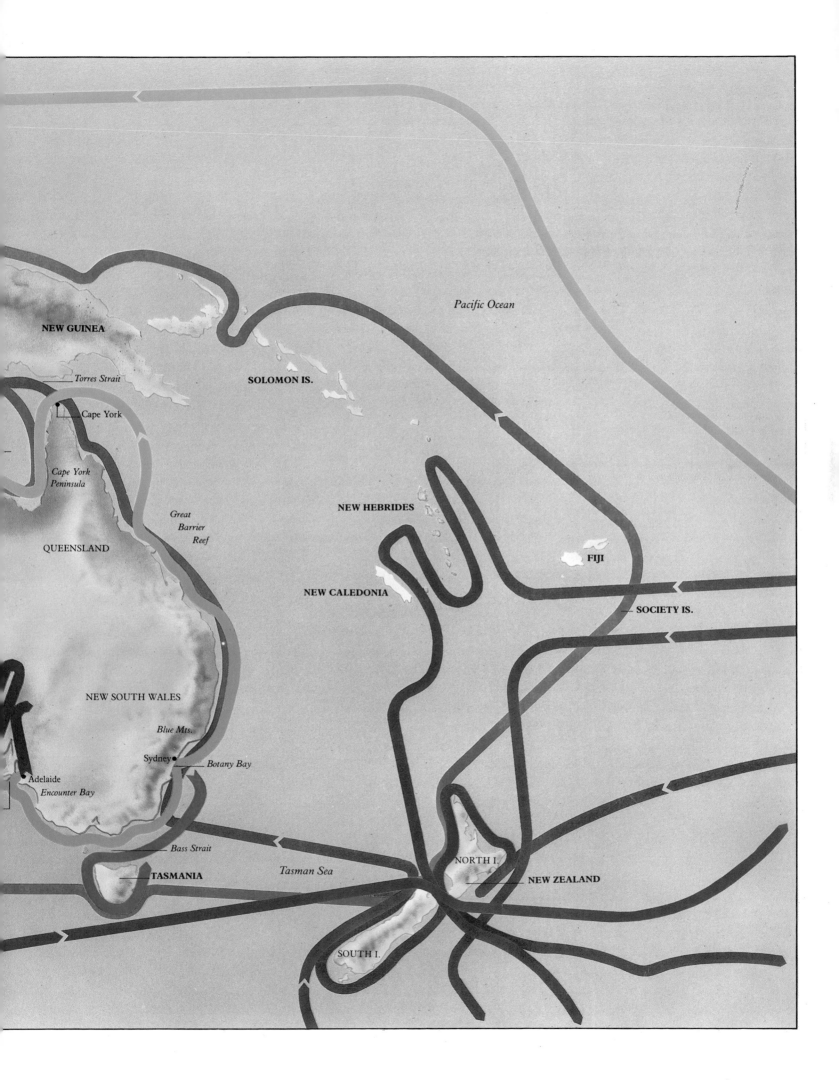

NEW GUINEA

Torres Strait

Cape York

Cape York
Peninsula

QUEENSLAND

Great
Barrier
Reef

NEW SOUTH WALES

Blue Mts.

Sydney •

Botany Bay

Adelaide

Encounter Bay

Bass Strait

TASMANIA

Tasman Sea

SOLOMON IS.

Pacific Ocean

NEW HEBRIDES

NEW CALEDONIA

FIJI

SOCIETY IS.

NORTH I.

NEW ZEALAND

SOUTH I.

Da Gama and Magellan: pioneer and circumnavigator

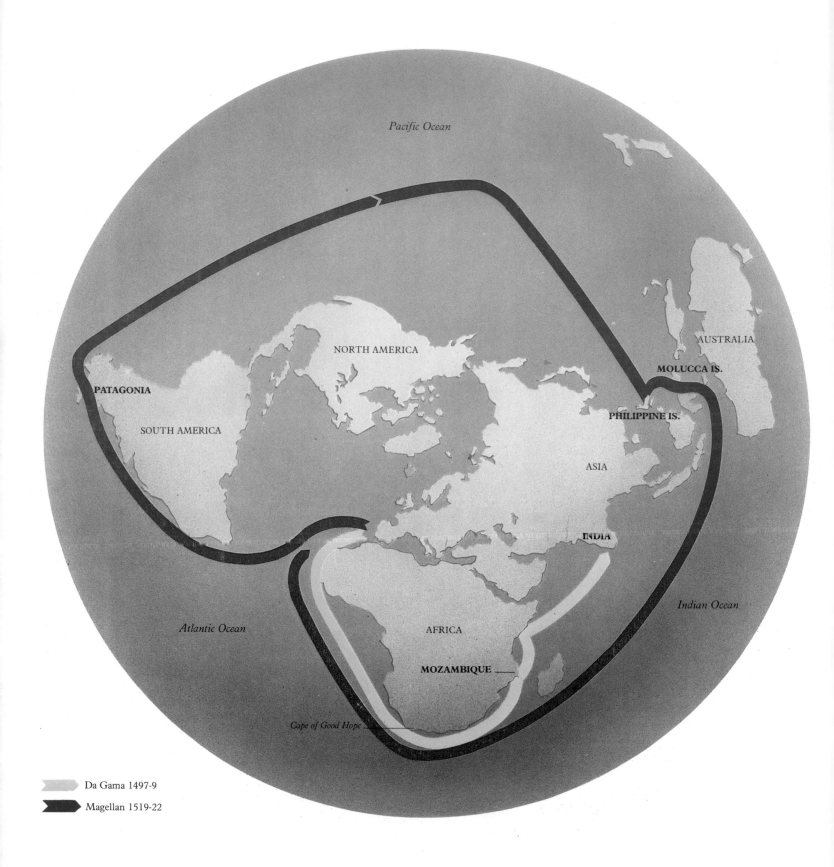

Pacific Ocean

NORTH AMERICA

AUSTRALIA

MOLUCCA IS.

PATAGONIA

PHILIPPINE IS.

SOUTH AMERICA

ASIA

INDIA

Indian Ocean

Atlantic Ocean

AFRICA

MOZAMBIQUE

Cape of Good Hope

Da Gama 1497-9

Magellan 1519-22

Vasco da Gama

(*c*1460 – 1521)

When Christopher Columbus told King John of Portugal of his discoveries – which he supposed to be Asia – in 1493, the king first conceived a plan to claim the new lands for Portugal. However the pope issued a bull granting all lands discovered west and south of Spain to the Spanish king and queen. Portugal's only option, then, was to set out *eastwards* to find a sea-route to the riches of India. In 1487 Bartholomew Diaz had rounded the Cape of Good Hope, proving that there was a sea-route eastwards around the southern tip of Africa. The new king, Manoel I, therefore commanded an expedition to sail without delay, under the command of Vasco da Gama.

Da Gama was born in the small port of Sines in south-west Portugal, the third son of a nobleman. As a young man he saw 'service in the fleets and in maritime affairs' and, though details of his early life and education are not known, he somehow acquired a good knowledge of mathematics and navigation.

A fleet of four ships, robust enough to withstand high seas at the Cape, was fitted out in 1497 for the voyage. Da Gama's ship was the *São Gabriel*, and the *São Rafael* was captained by his brother, Paolo. Between 140 and 170 men (the exact number is unknown), some of them convicted criminals, went on the meticulously planned expedition. Half of them were to die on the voyage. On 8 July 1497, with every blessing the Church and king had it in their power to bestow, the ships slipped down the Tagus and stood out to sea for India, via the Cape Verde Islands and Sierra Leone. Instead of hugging the African mainland, da Gama swung out to the south and west in order to avoid the doldrums and the Guinea current, returning to the coast just above the Cape of Good Hope. Rounding it, by mid-December he was beyond the Great Fish River, the limit reached by his pioneering predecessor, Bartholomew Diaz, and crossing unknown, seemingly boundless, seas.

By this time, however, the expedition was stricken by the disease to which sailors were particularly vulnerable – scurvy, a miserable affliction caused (though no one knew it then) by a vitamin deficiency through lack of fresh food. Da Gama advised his men to use the drastic remedies believed in at the time: cutting out gangrenous sores with a knife and rubbing bleeding gums with urine. Thirty men died, suppurating in agony.

Fierce storms and contrary currents made their progress up the west coast of Africa slow, but the sailors' suffering was relieved by their arrival on 24 February 1498 in Mozambique, where fresh food could be procured. They were now in the Arab sphere of influence, and the weary, rough sailors gaped at the riches they saw. One of the party wrote:

They all wear toucas, with borders of silk embroidered in gold. They are merchants, and have transactions with white Moors, four of whose vessels were at the time in the port, laden with gold, silver, cloves, pepper, ginger and silver rings, as also quantities of pearls, jewels, and rubies, all of which articles are used by the people of this country ... and we were told that further on, where we were going to, they abounded, and that precious stones, pearls and spices were so plentiful that there was no need to purchase them, as they could be collected in baskets.

On the whole their reception was friendly, but it was soon marred by some ugly incidents for which the Portuguese were largely responsible: an old Arab picked up in a boat was tortured even before questioning; and at Mombasa (now in Kenya) two men were tortured with boiling oil until they confessed that there was a plot afoot to attack the ship. The attack, which duly came, was beaten off and was only one unfortunate incident between Muslims and Christians. 'These dogs tried many another knavery on us,' wrote the anonymous chronicler of the expedition, in the spirit of the times, 'but Our Lord did not will them to succeed, because they did not believe in Him.'

On 14 April they reached Malindi (on the

Left The great and ruthless da Gama.

Previous page The cross marks Vasco da Gama's landfall north of Malindi, Kenya. On their second visit, da Gama's men were suffering from the ravages of scurvy after a three-month voyage from Calicut and were about to turn back, when a favourable wind arose to blow them onwards.

Surate

coast of Kenya) and were given a friendly welcome by the king, whose court was as opulent as Mozambique's:

The king wore a robe of damask trimmed with green satin and a rich touca. He was seated on two cushioned chairs of bronze, beneath a round sunshade of crimson satin attached to a pole. ... There were many players on arafils, and two trumpets of ivory, richly carved and the size of a man, which were blown from a hole in the side, and made sweet harmony with the arafils.

After being fêted for nine days they took on board a pilot and set off across the Indian Ocean on the main purpose of the expedition – to find India. In May 1498 they sighted Calicut, the most important trading post in southern India, and the place they most wanted to reach. 'The devil take you! What brought *you* here?' was the first question some Muslim merchants asked. 'We are looking for Christians and spices,' replied da Gama. 'Why haven't the French, or Spaniards or Venetians sent ships before?' asked the merchants. 'Because the King of Portugal won't let them,' he said. It showed that the east knew more about Europe than Europe knew about the east.

When they went into a Hindu temple they thought they had found Christians. The mistake was mutual: Hindus coming aboard supposed that the Virgin Mary was a strange version of their own multi-armed goddess Devi. Da Gama stayed for three months, but difficulties with the poor quality of trade goods made a longer stay hazardous. Gold, silver, corals and scarlet cloth were what was wanted and da Gama failed to set up a Portuguese trading post. When he set sail for Portugal in August da Gama judged it expedient to take five or six Hindu hostages, explaining that he needed evidence of native people for his king; only a storm prevented the Calicut fleet from pursuing and attacking them for this last arrogant gesture.

During their three-month journey back across the Indian Ocean scurvy gained more and more of a hold. Another thirty sailors died, and the rest unwillingly took over their tasks. Discipline hung on a thread; there were constant threats of mutiny. In desperation, a council of officers decided to return to India but then a favourable wind arose, allowing them to make a landfall north of Malindi. The leaking *São Rafael* could no longer be manned, so she was set on fire and abandoned.

A gentle breeze wafted them past the Cape of Good Hope on 20 March, and at last the cool winds blew – and nearly froze the mariners. '*Now* what have you got to say about your past behaviour?' da Gama asked the gallant remnant of his men, assembling them on deck. 'Sir, we acted according to as

Above Arab merchants with a foothold in Surat, north of Bombay, tried in vain to fend off the Portuguese invaders; as shown by an illustration from *Livro da Estado da India Oriental* by Bocarro (1646).

83

TROPI CO DI CA N

MARDE INDIA

EQVI NOCTIAL

we are: you acted like as you are. Now, Sir,
on a day of much joy, it is in reason that we
should be pardoned.'

Da Gama reached Lisbon in September,
after a gruelling voyage of two years, with
300 days at sea. His success waş well
received in Portugal, naturally enough, but
when the news reached Venice, 'the pop-
ulace was thunderstruck and the wiser
among them regarded the news as the worst
they could have received' – indeed a new
shipping route round the cape spelled the
end of a near-monopoly of eastern trade for
the merchants of Venice.

Da Gama was heaped with money,
patents of nobility and honours including
the title 'Admiral of the Indian Sea'. In
1502 he again set sail for the Indies with ten

ships, together with two subsidiary expeditions of five ships each under his uncle
and his nephew. The journey out witnessed
one of the most frightful maritime mas-
sacres on record. Off Cannanore in south-
west India, da Gama, intent on using his
naval supremacy for plunder, lay in wait for
Arab spice ships. The *Meri* was returning
from Mecca with more than 200 men,
women and children aboard. Having looted
its stores, da Gama had the passengers and
crew locked in the hold and set the ship on
fire. As the *Meri* burned, the Portuguese
ships maintained a bombardment. Women
and children burst out on deck, calling on
Allah for deliverance, pleading for their
lives, even flinging babies into the sea. As
the flames died down da Gama ordered his

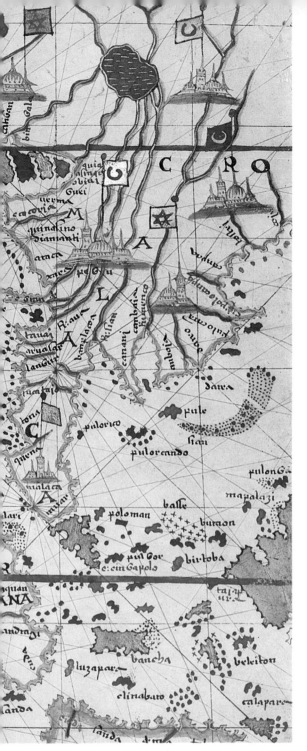

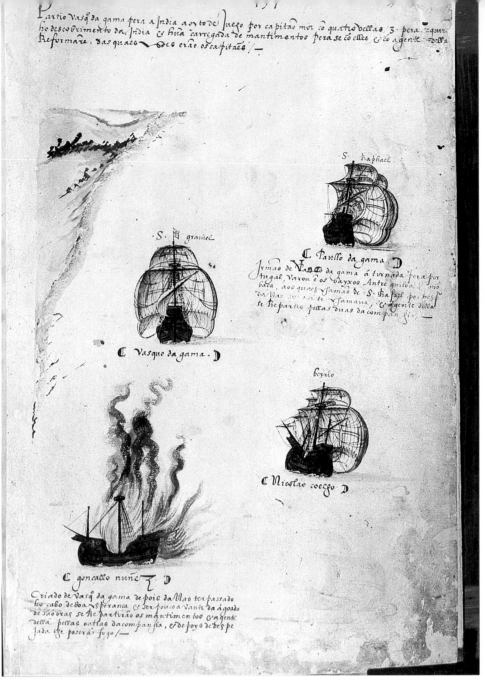

S. Rafael

S. grauiel

C Paullo da gama D

Irmão de Vasco da gama á tornada pera por tugal. Varou e os Bayxos Antre quilva & mo bâça. Aos quaes esanão de S. Rafael por tres. se Repartio pellas duas da companhia

C Vasquo da gama. D

boyão

C Nicolao coeego D

C goncallo nunẽ D

Criado de Vasq̃ da gama depois da Nao ter passado ho cabo de Boa Esperança & ser pouco a vante da agoada de São Bras se he partirão os mantimentos e a gente della pellas outras da companhia, & depois de despe jada se poserá fogo

men to leap on board and fire the ship all over again; and this went on for four days and nights, the fires being relit and requenched, again and again.

This awful affair was a prelude to da Gama's deeds at Calicut. Remembering how obstructive the Arab merchants had been before, he demanded that every Muslim in Calicut be deported. Snatching some thirty fishermen – obviously Hindus, not Muslims – who had come out in small boats to sell fish to the ships, he had them strung up. That night he ordered the corpses to be dismembered and thrown overboard to drift with the incoming tide onto the wharf, where shrieking families tried to identify their own by the few poor rags still on each mutilated, bobbing torso.

Feared and hated, da Gama returned to Portugal in 1503 and made his last voyage eastwards when he became governor of Portuguese India in 1524. His voyage to India had opened up a new epoch in Portugal's history. A country which had been a poor nation of fishermen and peasants now established trading supremacy in the Indian Ocean, and the rich Portuguese Empire flourished. But in Cochin, beyond the furthest point reached on his first voyage, he fell ill with tormenting boils, 'with such pain as deprived him of speech'. And there, on Christmas Eve, he died. Dressed in a mantle of the Order of Christ, his body was borne on the shoulders of monks of The Brotherhood of Mercy to their chapel. It was a long time before the body returned to Portugal. Cruel even by the harsh standards of his day, da Gama was nevertheless one of the greatest European explorers.

Above The ships of Vasco da Gama's fleet were crewed partly by convicted criminals. So many died of disease that the leaking *São Rafael* could no longer be manned, so she was set on fire and abandoned off Malindi.

85

Ferdinand Magellan

(1480 – 1521)

Left Ferdinand Magellan: a portrait by an unknown artist after another portrait, also by an unknown artist, now in the Uffizi Gallery, Florence.

The Portuguese kings and their governments towards the end of the fifteenth and start of the sixteenth centuries were not easily persuaded to support expeditions of discovery. Columbus, Cabot and Vespucci all tried and failed to gain backing for their voyages, and turned elsewhere. So did Ferdinand Magellan, Portuguese-born and bred, and Portuguese-trained in the East Indies. He went to Spain, took Spanish nationality, and petitioned the Spanish king, Charles V. He had picked the right moment, for the Portuguese had beaten Spain in her attempt to gain spices from the east, and while cargoes from the Moluccas were unloading at Lisbon, Spain had none. Magellan's Portuguese training, and his familiarity with the sea route to the Moluccas, could therefore be of great service to Spain. The sea route eastwards to the Moluccas was monopolized by the Portuguese, but Magellan persuaded the king to support his belief that there was a sea route *westwards* around the southern tip of South America, to which the Moluccas (in this he was mistaken) lay fairly close.

Magellan was given five ships, the *Trinidad, San Antonio, Concepción, Vittoria* and *Santiago*, about 270 men, and stores (including trade goods and a large and comprehensive supply of navigational instruments) and ammunition for two years. On 20 September 1519 he set sail from the mouth of the Guadalquivir in southern Spain. Sailing down the east coast of South America, the flotilla was becalmed for two months off the Guinea coast. Then, like a bluebottle thudding against a window-pane, Magellan tried to find some opening westward into the South Sea. Near Rio de Janeiro, the natives flocked down to the beach thinking that the five ships were sea-monsters, the small boats being their young. A king from a pack of cards was gleefully exchanged for five chickens – 'And they thought they had cheated me,' wrote Antonio Pigafetta, an Italian on board who kept a diary. At the River Plate, Magellan sailed up the estuary, thinking he had found a passage. Going on down south he anchored in the bay of Port St Julian for a winter of discontent, during which he crushed a mutiny by passing sentences of death and marooning.

Opposite A sixteenth-century map of South America showing contemporary ideas of the inhabitants (including cannibals and giants) and of the monsters lurking in the depths of the sea. Beneath the Patagonian giants can be seen the Straits of Magellan.

At last, in August 1520, the flotilla moved on southwards. It stopped in Patagonia, where Magellan's men thought the skins the natives wore on their feet were hoofs, and Magellan played a trick upon the visiting natives. Under guise of friendship he loaded two of them with gimcrack gifts, then clamped iron fetters on their legs. At first they jingled them delightedly, but delight turned to dismay when they were bundled off below-decks as prisoners for the human zoo Magellan hoped to bring back with him to Spain.

After nearly two months of searching they found the Cape of the Eleven Thousand Virgins of St Ursula where the coast turned directly west. Overcoming opposition from his men, made permanently semi-mutinous by the difficulties of the voyage, Magellan sent the *Concepción* and the *San Antonio* ahead to reconnoitre. They were swept away by a fierce storm, but returned two days later with news of the entrance to a passage. It was only Magellan's determination that forced the little fleet into the strait. 'Though we have nothing left to eat but the leather wrappings from our masts, we shall go on,' he declared. It took thirty-eight days to thread a passage through 360 miles of inlets and

fjords in one of the most tempestuous waterways in the world. Midway, the *San Antonio's* crew mutinied and turned back to Spain, taking with them most of the expedition's supplies. That three ships, the *Trinidad*, the *Concepción* and the *Vittoria*, emerged into the Pacific was testament to Magellan's superb navigational skills.

The three small ships were now challenging the earth's greatest ocean, about to make one of the greatest sea passages ever made. Their troubles had barely begun. The sea was calm, so they named it the 'Pacific' and steered a course northwards. Now they were doomed to disappointment, for they had no idea of the vast stretch of water that separated them from the Moluccas. In January they sighted their first land: it was an island, barren and empty, later called Disappointment Island. For nearly a hundred days they were out of sight of land, and conditions must have become unimaginably bad. By the time they reached Guam in the Marianas the crew were indeed eating leather from the masts, and worm-ridden, rat-fouled biscuits; rats had become the standard for barter and what remained of their water stank of the bilges. Inevitably, scurvy broke out: nineteen men died, and dozens fell ill.

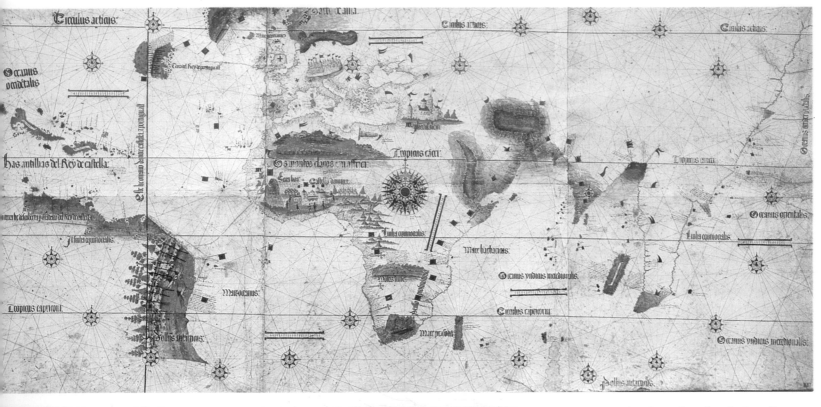

Above On the ceiling of a church at Cebu in the Philippines Magellan is seen planting a cross to commemorate the baptism of the island's first Christian convert.

Top The Cantin world map of 1502 shows the spheres of influence agreed in the Treaty of Tordesillas.

It was March when they landed at Guam, and then sailed on to the Philippines and Cebu, where they were well received. Magellan's religious zeal, however, proved fatal. He insisted on subjugating and baptizing the chieftains of Cebu and the neighbouring islands. On the island of Mactan he met opposition; he invaded it, causing a pointless skirmish in which he and about forty of his men were killed.

The survivors (115 men out of an original 237) finally managed to get away in two ships, burning the third. At last the Moluccas, Magellan's goal, were reached, on 8 November 1521. One of the ships, the *Trinidad*, was abandoned, leaking, at Tidore and captured by the Portuguese, whilst the *Vittoria* was loaded to the gunwhales with cloves. Of the remaining crew, more died when scurvy struck again on the nine-month voyage home round Africa; and the Portuguese imprisoned others in the Cape Verde Islands. Only seventeen Europeans and four natives, under the command of Sebastian del Cano, returned to Seville. The *Vittoria*, the only ship left out of the original fleet, was leaking badly, and barely limped into harbour. The value of her cargo of cloves was enough to pay for the whole venture after all losses had been taken into account.

In the three years since they had left Spain, del Cano and Magellan before him had displayed great skill as navigators and leaders, and the men who survived were the first circumnavigators of the world.

Abel Tasman

(*c*1603 – 59)

Previous page The first flotilla of the Netherlands Company of Far Lands sailed in 1595, five years before the founding of the English East India Company. This painting of the *Return of the Dutch East India Fleet* is by Van Ertvelt.

Below Tasman with his wife and child. He could not have been altogether a model husband, for on his return to Amsterdam in 1637 his first wife cut him completely out of her will. His second wife, when widowed by his death, married again within eighteen months, even though she had to do it from her sickbed.

Hating their Spanish overlords (with whom they were at war until 1648) the Dutch were as ready as the English to plunder the ships of the Spanish bullion fleets, and just as capable and ruthless in doing so. In trade they excelled. With their Company of Far Lands, founded in 1595 and later to become the Dutch East India Company, the Dutch pushed their way into Java, Malabar, Amboyna, Malacca and the Moluccas, evicting the Spaniards and the Portuguese in the process. Amsterdam, the Dutch capital and the hub from which all spokes of commerce radiated out, became the richest city on earth.

The spice empire the Dutch established in the East Indies was the ideal base from which to search for 'Terra Australis', the eagerly postulated southern continent which many people believed to exist, but which no one had seen. Dutchmen had already made inconclusive and un-connected voyages along the north, south and west coasts, but Abel Tasman was the first to make a voyage all around the southern continent.

Tasman, born in humble circumstances in Groningen, would have seen little evidence of riches in the first years of his life. He went to sea as an ordinary sailor, and as such went out to Batavia (Jakarta) in the East Indies, rising to mate and then master within two years. By 1634 he was skipper of the *Mocha*, trading out of Amboyna, and by the following year he was a *commandeur*, a minor sort of admiral.

His first voyage of exploration was in 1639, as second-in-command to Mathijs Quast. Their object was to search for an outpost of Cathay reputed to be 'a very great country or island, rich without measure in gold and silver and inhabited by civilised and friendly people', which was said to lie to the east in latitude $37\frac{1}{2}°$ north. They sailed north of the Philippines to the Bonin Islands, and on towards Japan. Then they turned east and sailed 2000 miles out into the Pacific, losing half the crew through sickness but finding nothing.

By distinguishing himself in the service of the Dutch East India Company, Tasman brought himself to the notice of Governor-General Van Diemen, who supported Tasman's project to sail further south than anyone had yet been in the Indian Ocean, to discover whether the southern continent reached down as far as the land mass of the Antarctic.

At one time the southern side of the Straits of Magellan, Tierra del Fuego, had been thought perhaps to be the northern tip of that eagerly postulated place. But Drake had proved otherwise by sailing south of it. Perhaps its western boundary was the land from Cape York (in northern Queensland) on the north, to the Great Australian Bight on the south, traced by Dutch ships between 1616 and 1628. Van Diemen tried to learn more during the next decade, with limited success. Tasman's great voyage of discovery in 1642 was the next logical step.

He set out in August, with two ships, the *Heemskerk* and the *Zeehaen*, bound for Mauritius. Keeping a southerly course into the Roaring Forties (westerly winds which blow round the earth in latitudes 40° to 50°S, uninterrupted by land), they reached the Great Australian Bight, and there Tasman invited a council of officers to discuss what they should do next; this meant floating a barrel of notes and votes between ships. By 24 November their new course had brought them to the west coast of Tasmania, off the south-east coast of Australia. They called it Van Diemen's Land. A strong swell made it difficult for Tasman himself to get ashore to take formal possession of the land, so the ship's carpenter swam through the surf and planted their flag firmly on dry land.

The prevalence of a wind blowing from the north-west took them on an eastward course and led to a landfall on the west coast of South Island, New Zealand. Had they

been blown north-east they would have passed the Bass Strait separating Tasmania from Australia, and perhaps have found Terra Australis. In the manner of all explorers, they conferred new names on places; a bay to the north was called 'Massacre Bay' after an attack by Maoris. This was their first sight of the warlike native people. Tasman left New Zealand, believing he had found the west coast of the 'unknown south land'.

Sailing on north-east, they discovered Tonga and Fiji, returning to Batavia via New Guinea in June 1643. In a voyage of more than 5000 miles Tasman had proved that Australia was not connected to the south polar mass, and that it was entirely surrounded by water. He had sailed right round Australia without ever seeing it. The Dutch East India Company, however, was more interested in commercial applications of Tasman's expedition, and finding there were no riches or people to exploit, received him coolly: Tasman 'had been to some extent remiss in investigating the situation, conformation and nature of the lands and peoples discovered, and left the main part of this task to be executed by some more inquisitive successor.'

Tasman's second expedition, of three ships, left Batavia a year later, with specific instructions (which he did not follow) to search for a strait between Terra Australis and New Guinea. He charted the western and northern coast of Australia up to the Torres Strait and followed the east coast to latitude 22° south. The results of the voyage were again disappointing to his backers, the East India Company, who had hoped he would discover lands of potential riches; but as Governor Van Diemen commented resignedly: 'The discovery of new countries is not work for everyone.'

The rest of Tasman's life was spent in relative obscurity: in 1652 he was sent to attack a Spanish bullion fleet at Manilla. He was unsuccessful and the expedition proved personally disastrous. He'd been making good cheer at a monastery and returned to find two of his sailors, supposed to be confined to camp, wandering freely about outside. In a fit of fury he strung one of the men up to a tree, feet resting on a bench,

Above Tasman's journal of his voyage of 1642–3 contained various charmingly naïve woodcuts showing native life in New Guinea and New Zealand.

Below 'Terra Australis', that eagerly postulated but wholly imaginary continent required in the interests of symmetry to balance the Americas, forms part of Mercator's Atlas of 1595.

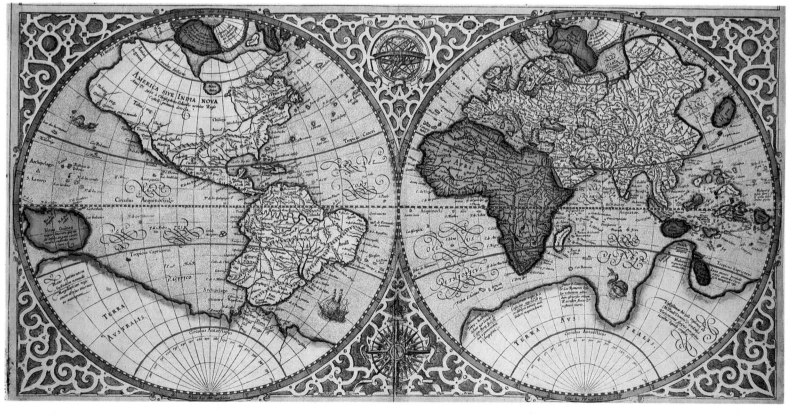

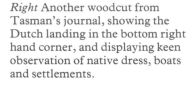

Right Another woodcut from Tasman's journal, showing the Dutch landing in the bottom right hand corner, and displaying keen observation of native dress, boats and settlements.

Below The market in Batavia (Jakarta) betrays strong Dutch colonial influence.

then kicked the bench away before starting on the other (who, fortunately, was released just in time by his second-in-command). On his return, Tasman was tried for unreasonable conduct. He was well and truly punished, suspended from office, ordered to pay a fine to the sailor's family, sacked from the post of Elder and finally made 'to stand barehead in open Court, and publicly declare that he had unjustly and unlawfully, without form of trial, of his own mere pleasure, and with his own hand, infamously executed the aforesaid innocent'.

He was only gradually reinstated, and became a merchant at Batavia, where he died in 1659. With him died Dutch exploration for the rest of the century, for while the greatness of his voyage went unrecognized, the information he brought back about the disposition of the islands about Australia was enough to satisfy Dutch curiosity for the next fifty years.

James Cook
(1728 – 79)

Above The celebrated portrait of
Captain Cook by Nathaniel Dance
hardly suggests a hasty temper, yet
Cook was supposed to be intolerant
of contradiction. He was certainly
possessed of a great deal of
commonsense as far as the welfare of
his crew was concerned.

Previous page Oo-oai-tepeha Bay,
Tahiti – an idyllic picture of Captain
Cook's ships by William Hodges.
Tahiti, presumed discovered by
Quiros in 1606, visited by Wallis in
1767 and by Bougainville a year
later, was called *La nouvelle Cythère*
and thought to be the home of the
Noble Savage.

The eighteenth century was an age of
scientific enquiry, and the great voyages of
James Cook were embarked upon in that
spirit. In 1768 the Royal Society appointed
him commander of an expedition to the
Pacific to chart the course of the planet
Venus across the sun.

Cook was an unusual man to be accorded
such distinction. Forty years old in 1768, he
was one of nine children of a Yorkshire
farmhand. In his teens he was bound
apprentice in a general store near Whitby,
but soon left to ply ships in the local coal
trade. He earned quick promotion, but
volunteered for the Royal Navy and saw
service in the Seven Years War (1756–63)
with France; during the war he distin-
guished himself by the ability, completely
self-taught, with which he charted the St
Lawrence River, thereby contributing to
the success of General Wolfe's landing
there. In the 1760s a marine survey of
Newfoundland and Labrador and his careful observation of a solar eclipse enhanced
his reputation for scientific accuracy. It was
this that led to his departure, in 1768, on
one of the greatest voyages of discovery in
history. This modest Yorkshireman had

already proved himself a great seaman,
navigator and cartographer; he was now to
become a great explorer.

In spite of the portraits there is some
doubt about Cook's appearance, particularly his head. According to Samwell it
was 'small with small eyes', yet the famous
portrait by Dance showed a large head with
broad, rather thick features. His character,
as described by others, remains controversial. Samwell described him as bash-
ful. Midshipman Trevenen spoke of his
taste as being 'the coarsest, surely, that ever
mortal was endowed with'. Zimmerman
described him as 'so hasty tempered that
the least contradiction on the part of an
officer or sailor made him very angry'. Yet
he apparently never swore. If an indistinct
picture emerges it is because his self-taught
erudition and his meticulous outlook so
balanced the impetuous side of his character that he avoided the larger-than-life
aspect characteristic of many great men.

With Joseph Banks, a rich and talented
natural scientist, Daniel Solander, a
Swedish naturalist, and Charles Green, the
Royal Society's official astronomer, Cook
set sail from Plymouth in August 1768 for
the South Seas. His ship was the
Endeavour, a small but sturdy Whitby coal-
ship, and his instructions were, having
observed Venus, to find the southern
continent, 'Terra Australis'.

It was January before they reached
Tierra del Fuego, at the southern tip of
South America. There they landed in gales
and bitter cold to collect botanical specimens; out for a walk with companions in
the intense cold, Dr Solander excelled
himself: 'Keep walking!' he told them
earnestly. 'Whoever sits down will sleep;
and whoever sleeps will wake no more!' So
of course it had to be the learned doctor
himself who first 'insisted upon being
suffered to repose', but this the others
would not allow.

They rounded Cape Horn in remarkably
calm seas, and in April they arrived in
Tahiti, where Cook laid down scrupulous
rules of conduct for the building of a fort
from which to observe the famous 'transit
of Venus' (which was duly observed, in a
cloudless sky, at its appointed time). He
insisted on paying for everything and
obtained permission before even cutting
down a tree. However, the observatory was
sensibly built within range of the
Endeavour's guns.

Pilfering was a major problem. One of
Cook's guards shot into a crowd of
Tahitians and killed a thief; and later, the

ship's butcher tried to force a Tahitian girl to give him her stone axe, threatening to kill her if she didn't. Cook decided the time had come to make an example. When Tahitians came on board ship he had the butcher stripped, tied to the rigging, and beaten in front of the visitors. As the first lash decended they showed great agitation and tried to get the punishment stopped. When they could not they burst into tears. But Cook remained inflexible; the lashing continued. At least it was his own man being punished. Later, when two marines deserted, Cook thought nothing of detaining in the fort some chiefs (including the stout 'princess' Oberea, who had previously feasted Mr Banks, to whom she took a particular fancy, on baked dog), until the unwilling natives surrendered the marines, who received two dozen lashes each. It was remarkable for a European explorer of Cook's time to show such a high-principled concern for justice in the dealings of his men with native populations. He evidently impressed the Tahitians, for in spite of the tensions, several of them wanted to be taken away by Cook. A chief called Tupia and his servant were the successful applicants, and there was much lamentation when the party set sail in July.

As they sailed on through the South Seas, Tupia was to prove useful as an interpreter. Over two months and 1600 miles after leaving the Society Islands they landed in New Zealand, where they found hostile Maoris and evidence of cannibalism. The next five months, until March 1770, they spent circumnavigating both North and South Island, thus establishing the fact that New Zealand could not be part of Terra Australis. They travelled 2400 miles and established that the land was fertile and suitable for colonization.

Now Cook struck out on a new route; instead of sailing with the westerly winds round Cape Horn which, in high latitudes, with winter approaching, would have been extremely dangerous, he decided to return home by way of the East Indies, striking westwards across the Tasman Sea. The route brought the *Endeavour*, in April 1770, to the south-east coast of Australia, which Cook named New South Wales, and on 28 April the little ship came to anchor in a bay 'which appeared to be tollerably well sheltered'. The botanists on board were delighted with the variety of plant life around the bay, and so Cook named it Botany Bay. The natives they encountered here, the first Aborigines they had seen, had dark, almost black, skins and spoke a

Above In *Captain Cook's first landing in the New Hebrides, Malicollo* William Hodges succeeded in suggesting that the natives of the South Seas were really just brown Europeans.

Below J. Webber depicted Maoris in Queen Charlotte's Sound as long and lean.

dissonant language meaningless to Tupia. They brandished spears and were not mollified by having beads, nails 'and other trifles' thrown at them. Small shot drove them away, and gifts in their tree-bark shelters were ignored.

The crew stayed for eight days, feasting on stingray, and then set off north along the 2000-mile east coast of Australia. Conducting a detailed survey, Cook managed successfully to navigate the Great Barrier Reef, one of the most treacherous stretches of sea in the world. On 11 June, however, the *Endeavour* struck the reef, and only Cook's skill in refloating her and mending an underwater leak at sea saved her from sinking.

By the end of August the expedition had negotiated the passage between New Guinea and Australia, doubling the north-eastern tip of Australia, and was in open sea, well on its way to Batavia (Jakarta), which it reached on 10 October 1770.

By this time nearly everybody on board was suffering from dysentery or malaria. In previous centuries many of the crew on such a long voyage would undoubtedly have sickened and died of scurvy. But by Cook's time new understanding had shown the importance of fresh fruit and vegetables in combating scurvy. Like all captains on long sea journeys, Cook feared scurvy above all else, and in his humanitarian concern for the health of his crew introduced a radical new diet and much improved standards of cleanliness. He was prepared if necessary to force his diet on a reluctant crew, in spite of their objections. As he himself wrote:

Such are the Tempers and dispositions of Seamen in general that whatever you give them out of the common way altho it be ever so much for their own good yet it will not go down with them and you will hear nothing but murmurings against the Man that first invented it; but the Moment they see their Superiors set a Value upon it, it becomes the finest stuff in the World and the inventor a damn'd honest fellow.

After his second voyage he admitted: 'Few men have introduced into their ships more novelties in the way of victuals and drink than I have done,' and claimed that in so doing he had kept his people 'generally speaking free from that dreadful distemper the scurvy.'

Cook did not invent the fresh food method of treatment. The Admiralty had conducted experiments more than twenty years earlier. But Cook's insistence on bringing barrels of citrus juice, sauerkraut and other supposed remedies, combined

Above On his third voyage, Cook sailed as far into the Arctic as Icy Cape, Alaska. Icebergs and pack-ice stopped him from going any further into the North-west Passage.

Above right On his first voyage, Cook had called in at Tierra del Fuego, where he found specimens of *Apium antarcticum*. Cook assumed that all fresh green plants helped to combat scurvy because of some mysterious 'principle' in them. He was right: the 'principle' is called Vitamin C, and it was not synthesized until after the First World War.

Previous page *Cape Stevens* by William Hodges.

with his efforts to procure fresh food wherever he could, undoubtedly amounted to real innovation.

Seven of the crew died at Batavia, and at Cape Town Cook had to engage more crew members for the passage home. In June 1771 they passed Beachy Head, having been absent almost three years.

Cook's second voyage, between July 1772 and July 1775, was to discover once and for all whether Terra Australis existed. In two ships, the *Resolution*, another old Whitby coal-ship, and the *Adventure*, and again accompanied by numerous scientists, Cook sailed from Cape Town to the southern latitudes, crossing the Antarctic Circle, and working his way eastwards to a point south of New Zealand, thus proving to his own absolute satisfaction that Terra Australis was a myth. He reached latitude 71° south, being of the opinion that the ice with which he was surrounded 'extended quite to the pole, or, perhaps joined to some land, to which it had been fixed from the earliest times'. Soon afterwards, Cook was afflicted with 'a bilious cholic'. As he recovered he craved fresh meat. There being none on board, 'a favourite dog belonging to Mr Forster' was killed and served up at table.

In August 1773 they reached Tahiti and Tonga, took on fresh supplies, and in November Cook set off again into the Antarctic. The cold the expedition experienced was bitter: 'Our ropes were like wires, Sails like boards or plates of Metal,' wrote Cook. Even in such conditions the crew again plunged south into the ice fields, which eventually blocked their passage in the Amundsen Sea.

Returning north, they discovered Easter Island, with its strange statues, before returning to Tahiti, Cape Horn and home. On 29 July 1775 Cook reached Plymouth, having sailed 70,000 miles in three years, on an expedition which was the first to sail round the world from west to east. On his return he was made a fellow of the Royal Society and was given the Copley Gold Medal, one of its highest honours.

He was quickly off on another voyage, this time to probe the North-west Passage (a passage from the Pacific to the Atlantic round North America) from the Alaskan end, west to east. For this he took two ships (one of them being the *Resolution*) and most of the same men from his second voyage. Rounding the Cape of Good Hope he visited Tasmania and New Zealand, returning once more to Tahiti. From the Sandwich Islands (now the Hawaiian Islands), he moved north along the west coast of North America, zigzagging his way through the Bering Strait, until he reached Icy Cape in northern Alaska. There he met ice as compact as a wall, twelve feet high and higher to the north. August was drawing to an end: the Arctic winter was already beginning. Cook retreated south and returned to the Sandwich Islands.

This time he was received with shouting and singing but also with pilfering. The armourers' tongs and chisels were stolen. In the night, even a small boat mysteriously went adrift. Resolved to make an example he planned to abduct the king and keep him as hostage against the return of the stolen boat. He therefore took an armed party ashore with him in a pinnace. On reaching the king's 'palace' he took the old man by the hand 'in a friendly manner' and insisted he return with them to the ship. The king consented, but his wife objected strenuously, and at the waterfront threw her arms round his neck to detain him, shrieking that he would be put to death if he set foot on board the foreign ships. Stones were flung, and muskets discharged while Cook was seen making for the pinnace, holding his left hand against the back of his head to ward off missiles. He was clubbed and stabbed within sight of a boatful of his own men; and his body was slashed and stabbed again on the beach before being carried off in triumph. Some parts of his dismembered corpse were returned to Captain Clerke, who had taken over command. But from then on and for the next fifty years, a wicker basket covered in red feathers was annually paraded around the island: in it was said to be what really remained of Captain James Cook. The practice continued until the islanders were converted to Christianity.

In eleven years Cook had made three great voyages around the world, discovering several previously unknown cultures and opening up large areas of the Pacific Ocean. In so doing he had set new, higher standards of scientific accuracy, carography, navigation and the general welfare of crews and native peoples alike.

Below Cook was killed in the Sandwich Islands (Hawaii) within sight of his own men. Six chiefs were killed in the mêlée. 'Some of your best friends,' said Chief Eappo cryptically, as he brought the remains of Cook's feet to his successor, Captain Clerke.

Matthew Flinders

(1774 – 1814)

In 1788 the first British convicts and settlers arrived at Botany Bay. Australia had been chosen as the new destination for transportees now that America, where they had previously been shipped, had won independence. The naturalist Sir Joseph Banks, who had sailed with Cook, supported the idea, pointing out the added advantage that the interior seemed rich in flax and timber, both of which were needed by Britain to maintain her naval superiority over the French.

Cook had charted the coastline of Australia, but the three million square miles of interior was still completely unmapped. The first settlers, however, found that natural barriers like the Blue Mountains blocked all routes from Botany Bay to the interior. Exploration from the land base therefore seemed impossible; the only alternative was to explore from the sea.

By coincidence the ship which brought New South Wales a new governor at this time also brought two young seamen with experience of amateur exploration: George Bass and Matthew Flinders.

The son of a Lincolnshire doctor, Flinders determined to be an explorer from the time that he read Daniel Defoe's *Robinson Crusoe*. 'I burned to have adventures of my own,' he declared. A short, slight young man, with a stern expression, he became a conscientious naval officer. In 1791 he joined the infamous Captain Bligh on one of his journeys to transport breadfruit from Tahiti to Jamaica. On this voyage Bligh nearly provoked a second mutiny like that on the *Bounty* by depriving the crew of fresh water in order to water the breadfruit with it.

It was in 1795 that Flinders began his exploration of the Australian coastline, starting, with Bass, in the *Tom Thumb*, a little boat only eight feet long. Two years later he and Bass, in an open whaleboat, circumnavigated Tasmania, discovering the passage between Australia and Tasmania which they called the Bass Strait, and finally proving that Tasmania was not part of the mainland.

Now Sir Joseph Banks had Flinders earmarked for the command of the leaky, defective *Investigator*, and the task of exploring the southern coast of Australia. Flinders might have had Mungo Park, the African explorer, with him as naturalist; but in the end Robert Brown came instead. William Westall was landscape draughtsman; Flinders' young cousin, John Franklin (who later became an Arctic explorer), managed to use the family

connection to gain a berth as midshipman, and Matthew's younger brother, Sam, was lieutenant. Flinders even managed to smuggle his wife aboard, but she was removed in disgrace when she was blamed for distracting her husband so that the *Investigator* ran aground on an uncharted sandbank. Sir Joseph Banks was far from pleased with his protégé's 'adventures to measures so contrary to the regulations'.

In December 1801 Flinders passed Cape Leeuwin and entered King George Sound coasting eastwards along the Great Australian Bight, christening place after place with good old Lincolnshire names. He made a survey of the Aborigines of the south-western coast and found they spoke a different language from those of New South Wales.

Once past Port Fowler he was sailing along a completely unexplored coast, and when it tended northwards, he thought he had found the entrance to a vast inland sea,

Above A miniature of Matthew Flinders: a short, slight man with a bouncing walk and rather stern expression: one of the few to hold his own with the infamous Captain Bligh of the *Bounty*.

Opposite For their circumnavigation of Australia, William Westall sailed with Captain Flinders as official artist. This is his view of Cape Townsend and the islands in Shoalwater Bay.

Above William Westall's painting of Government House, Sydney, in Flinder's day.

Below *Snake at Thistle Island* (William Westall). When Sir John Franklin, who as a young man sailed round Australia with Flinders, eventually became Governor of Van Diemen's Land, his wife Jane offered a reward of a shilling for every snake's head handed in to the police. The response proved so overwhelming she soon had to discontinue her bounty.

which many believed existed in the interior. In eager anticipation he followed the coast northwards for 200 miles, only to find it narrowing rapidly. He had discovered Spencer Gulf which eats deep into the interior. Flinders took the opportunity to explore the hinterland, as Robert Brown collected botanical specimens, William Westall sketched and John Franklin made it his business to annex a part of South Australia for England – an action later to be commemorated with an obelisk.

He carried along the coast to Kangaroo Island, named after the numerous kangaroos which inhabited it, and up and down Gulf St Vincent. It was near here, in Encounter Bay, that Flinders encountered a Frenchman, Baudin, on his ship the *Géographe*, plying westwards with her crew suffering dreadfully from scurvy. Baudin was under orders from Napoleon, with whom Britain was at war, and Flinders therefore prepared for action. However, the two ships passed amicably; little did Flinders know then that many of his discoveries were later to be claimed by the French as their own.

By the time they arrived in Port Jackson (Sydney), their survey of the south coast complete, Flinders and his crew were also suffering from scurvy, but the *Investigator* was suffering even more from decay. He had to put up with it: 'Better an old tub than none at all,' he said. After some repairs had been made, the ship sailed north to the Gulf of Carpentaria, by way of the Great Barrier Reef; channelling through it was like 'threading a needle'. Nothing more could be done for the *Investigator* at the Dutch port of Koepang, on the island of Timor, so Flinders carried on, heading down the west coast of Australia and back around to Sydney – having circumnavigated Australia in a vessel through which anyone could easily have poked a hole with a stick.

This success preceded a catalogue of disasters. On his way back to England in the *Porpoise* Flinders, technically not in command as he was writing an account of his explorations, was shipwrecked and found himself deposited on a low sandbank, fifty feet wide and 900 feet long, together with his cousin Franklin, his brother Sam, and some of the crew. Flinders decided to make for Sydney in the *Porpoise's* six-oared cutter – fourteen persons for a journey of 800 miles with provisions for a week. It took them thirteen days to reach port.

This was not all. He was given the *Cumberland*, a tiny schooner of twenty-nine tons, and he set off again for England. Almost immediately the pumps had to be set going; the *Cumberland* leaked as badly as the *Investigator*. They had to make for the French island of Mauritius for repairs, the very place he had been warned to avoid since France was then at war with England. Though passing ships were counted as being outside the war, the French were still 'the enemy' and likely to seize any excuse to be awkward if they could. However, the unfortunate Flinders had no choice. His passport identified him as the commander of the *Investigator*, not the *Cumberland*, and on this technicality he was detained by General de Caen and interrogated. The general felt there was something suspicious about an English explorer creeping about the French seas in such a tiny and decrepit vessel. The upshot was

that Flinders was detained on the island for six and a half years.

Back in England all possible influence was brought to bear on the French to relieve the plight of the punctilious captain, languishing in foreign parts. '*L'Affaire Flinders*' even reached the ears of the Empress Josephine, but Napoleon did not weaken. Meanwhile Flinders went on with writing his book.

An English blockade of Mauritius from 1809 and further representations finally resulted in his release in June the next year. His sword was handed back to him, and he was free to scramble back to England as best he could. He arrived, in the *Olympia*, in October 1810. He had been gone over nine years.

The Admiralty treated him shabbily, refusing to take his imprisonment into account when reckoning his promotion. He could not secure full pay whilst polishing up his book but had to be content with *ex gratia* grants. Though only forty when at last his book, *Voyage to Terra Australis*, went to press, he was already ill and worn out. He was unconscious when the first copy arrived on 18 July 1814. His hand was gently steered towards the record of his claim to fame, but he was too weak to turn the pages. Next day, as if still waiting for word from his publishers, he suddenly started up in bed and in a hoarse voice whispered 'My papers!', before relapsing into unconsciousness, from which he never recovered. As a final piece of ill fortune (though hardly surprising, as it cost twelve guineas – about £250 today) the book did not sell well.

Below The inhospitable, parched terrain of South Australia.

Edward John Eyre

(1815 – 1901)

Once Cook and Flinders had circumnavigated Australia, the vast continent was known in outline, but its interior was not so easily tamed; it was fiercely inhospitable, and the men who mapped it were some of the most intrepid explorers in history. As they moved into the interior they found it was impossible to follow any system of waterways, as the explorers of North America had been able to do. The Australian rivers often meandered for hundreds of miles, before dwindling away into nothing in the parched desert. Without the help of Aboriginal guides white men would never have survived their epic treks across thousands of miles of unwatered land. Only the Aborigines knew how to find water holes, and how to extract water from the roots of the sparse desert vegetation. The newcomers who braved the bush acquired a respect for Aboriginal ways of life and powers of adaptation, though their methods of subsistence (on fat white grubs and similar delicacies) were neither loved nor envied by the white colonizers. That the savage had much to teach the civilized seems obvious to us today; it was not so obvious in the middle of the last century. In his longing to understand natives, Edward Eyre was a pioneer as much as in his determination to explore the waterless country of the Great Australian Bight.

The son of an English clergyman, Eyre was born near Tavistock in Devon and attended Louth Grammar School in Lincolnshire. He went to Australia at the age of eighteen, with £400 in his pocket, to try his hand at sheep farming. Later he branched out as an 'overlander', transporting stock from Sydney to Adelaide. At about the same time he became resident magistrate at the Murray and 'protector of Aborigines'. On both counts he was well in with Governor Gawler of South Australia, which made it easier for him to arouse interest in his project to open up communications between the south and the west. Some money was raised to finance the scheme but the major portion of the cost came out of his own pocket.

Having been presented with 'a very handsome Union Jack, neatly worked in silk', he left Government House, Adelaide, in June 1840 to cheers of an escorting party of smart ladies in carriages and gentlemen on horseback. He headed north-west into the desert as far as Lake Torrens which he found completely dried up: '. . . the dry bed of the lake coated over with a crust of salt, formed one unbroken sheet of pure white, and glittering brilliantly in the sun.' There

was no hope of water in this direction so instead he struck westwards, but was defeated by the extreme heat, and forced to turn south towards the coast.

At Port Lincoln the murder of a white boy by natives prompted him to reflect on the general attitude of white to black: an attitude, he wrote, 'that leads them to think as little of firing at a black as at a bird, and which makes the number they have killed, or the atrocities that have attended the deeds, a matter for a tale, a jest, or boast at their pothouse revelries.'

The important phase of his journey was to begin from Fowlers Bay, where he met the cutter, *Hero*, which had brought him supplies. When the *Hero* came back with a message from Gawler entreating him to return, saying that they were completely satisfied with his explorations to date, Eyre remained adamant: he had decided to make a series of forced marches across the barren interior. With a foreman, Baxter, and three Aborigines (one of them a favourite servant named Wylie) he set out on 25 February 1841 for the thousand-mile journey to King George Sound, arond the Great Australian Bight. They took with them nine horses, one Timor pony, one foal and six sheep, for the main point of the expedition was to see how they would survive alone in the wild.

Above A portrait of Edward Eyre in 1845, from a coloured drawing presented to the South Australian Government by his grandson.

Opposite The unknown sand dunes of the Great Australian Bight nearly claimed the lives of Eyre and his companions.

Above An Australian Aborigine trudging home with a kangaroo he has killed with a spear. Eyre owed his survival to Aboriginal skills.

Below Aborigines in desperation frequently turned against the white colonizers.

The scrubby desert proved pitiless. Animals would not last long, that much was an obvious early lesson, but that men would die, too, was less predictable. What proved lethal were the common failings of humanity. Baxter, the overseer, wanted to turn back; but, unconvinced by Eyre's arguments, yet dominated by the stronger man's stronger will, he struggled on. As the nights became colder with the onset of winter and food supplies began to run out the Aborigines, too, longed to turn back and in their desperation hatched a plot. In the middle of the night of 28 April a shot rang out; Eyre found Baxter dead and two of the Aborigines gone. He was alone with Wylie. Luckily some ammunition, sewn up in a canvas bag, had been overlooked by the murderers. Now reduced to two, the expedition resumed its way. To make matters more sinister, on looking back Eyre saw 'two white objects moving stealthily in the scrub' – the murderers, covered by their blankets, following 'like wolves or bloodhounds on the track'. Even at such a juncture, Eyre was capable of reflecting: 'Nor would Europeans, perhaps, have acted better. In desperate circumstances men are apt to become discontented.'

At the beginning of June, all but mad from hunger and thirst after a trek of 600 miles, Eyre and Wylie were sitting on the sand of an unknown shore, gazing stoically out to sea, when Eyre saw a ship in the distance. Dragging himself along he found a fine large barque lying at anchor – a French whaler, the *Mississippi*, with an Englishman, Captain Rossiter, as skipper.

From 'Rossiter Bay', after two weeks recuperation on board, Eyre and Wylie resumed their journey. They at last reached their goal, Albany, Western Australia, on 8 July to the shouts and gasps of those who had presumed them dead. The overland route they had found was certainly not one that was suitable as a regular route for livestock, but its very impossibility made their achievement a most remarkable feat of courage and endurance.

Eyre's subsequent career was equally amazing. He was a well known figure when he went back to England in 1845, taking with him two Aboriginal boys, who were duly presented to Queen Victoria. One of the boys, 'proving of a vicious temper', was returned home. The other was sent to school under the care of the Quaker philanthropist Dr Hodgkin but died there of a pulmonary attack at the age of seventeen. Edward Eyre was made lieutenant-governor of New Zealand, and was then

sent to the West Indies, to become governor of Antigua, and subsequently acting-governor of Jamaica. He came up against a man, a member of the legislature, the Hon. Mr Gordon, described by the captain of the Confederate States schooner, *Happy-go-Lucky*, as 'a swell mulatto'. Trouble began when Eyre removed Gordon from the magistracy for (amongst other things) describing the clergy of the Church of England in Jamaica as 'the most immoral men in the whole island'. Gordon was a Jamaican patriot, an advocate of self-rule and the creation of a new 'West India Republic'. He planned to lead an uprising, and the plan included the purchase of the *Happy-go-Lucky* and all her arms and ammunition. 'People of St Thomas-in-the-East, you have been ground down too long already. Shake off your sloth!' declared an inflammatory pamphlet.

The uprising when it came was savage. The court house was attacked and men were hacked to pieces; twenty-two soldiers of the volunteer force – nearly the whole company – were murdered. Governor Eyre

declared martial law, instituted courts-martial and had Gordon and some of his followers hanged. Others were flogged and had their houses fired. The uprising was very soon at an end.

Her Majesty's Government congratulated Eyre on the way he had handled the rebellion; so did men such as Carlyle and Tennyson. But prolonged agitation by the Anti-Slavery Society led to the setting up of a royal commission, whose findings were that: 'The punishment of death was unnecessarily frequent, the floggings reckless, and the burning of houses wanton and cruel.' Eyre was removed from his post in 1866 and left Jamaica, according to one section of the press, 'to the warm cheers of Negroes shouting: "God bless Your Excellency!"' He arrived in England to face a private prosecution (which failed), and retired on a colonial governor's pension, having had the unusual distinction of being in one sphere the champion of the Aborigines and in another the oppressor of the West Indians.

Above Possibly the best way of seeing sand dunes south of Lake Eyre is from the air. There was good reason for calling the Great Australian Bight 'the handiwork of nature in her dotage'.

The Dark Continent

The coasts of Africa, 'the dark continent', were known in Europe long before the interior. After Queen Hatshepsut's trade mission to Punt, the earliest known Europeans to venture into Abyssinia were prompted as much by the theory that this might be the Christian kingdom of the mythical Prester John, as by the hope of discovering the source of the Queen of Sheba's riches.

Arab merchants were the real land pioneers, in quest of goods or African slaves. The slave trade was large and organized, and the slavers, when not black, were Arabs, themselves living in lands on the periphery of Africa, well placed for buying forays. Such victims as survived the horrors of a slave caravan were sold in the bazaars for distribution further afield. Needless to say, Europeans were quick to exploit this disgraceful source of profit; and with a superior efficiency which made them excel in inhumanity.

The great explorers of the interior were untainted by such commerce, yet they often had to rely upon the good graces of those who dealt in slaves, Christian and Muslim traders who alone had contacts without which not even a start could be made. James Bruce, on his way to trace the source of the Blue Nile, was beholden to the Coptic Christian, Ras Michael of Tigré, who annually sent 500 women and children to Massawa where the Muslim ruler exacted a toll before passing them on. Mungo Park, braving the Niger on behalf of the African Association, had slaves as servants and relied on the good offices of *slatees*, the black merchants whose stock in trade was largely human.

African rivers offered a doubtful route into the interior, yet the Victorian English were obsessed with tracing the source of the Nile. Burton, Speke, Grant and the rest could not have advanced very far had they not made Zanzibar their base, and from there, with material help from the sultan, struck inland across Africa to the great lakes. South of Khartoum the river fans out into the Sudd swamp, a formidable barrier to the logical plan of following the course of the river along its banks from the lower reaches. The Sudd had baffled explorers since the days of the Emperor Nero. The Bakers were amongst those who at last managed to close some of the Nile gaps, but by that time steamers could penetrate the swamp and reach as far up the river as Gondokoro, near the modern town of Juba, and were only stopped from further progress by falls and rapids. Beyond these were the great lakes and the river's supposed source to the west, the 'Mountains of the Moon' shown in Ptolemy's second-century map and rediscovered by Stanley in 1888. Livingstone was in a class of his own; at first more missionary than explorer, and later more explorer than missionary.

For all its great rivers, Africa has many deserts. These have attracted travellers who have felt a kinship with the nomads, particularly with the Bedouin, whose lives they found to be harsh, yet somehow glamorous. It was a sentimental yearning based only loosely on an appreciation of the realities of desert life. Barth, Nachtigal and Burton, among others 'crazed with the spell of far Arabia', nevertheless faced and overcame the often appalling difficulties of travel through the forbidding sands.

River Gambia

SENEGAL

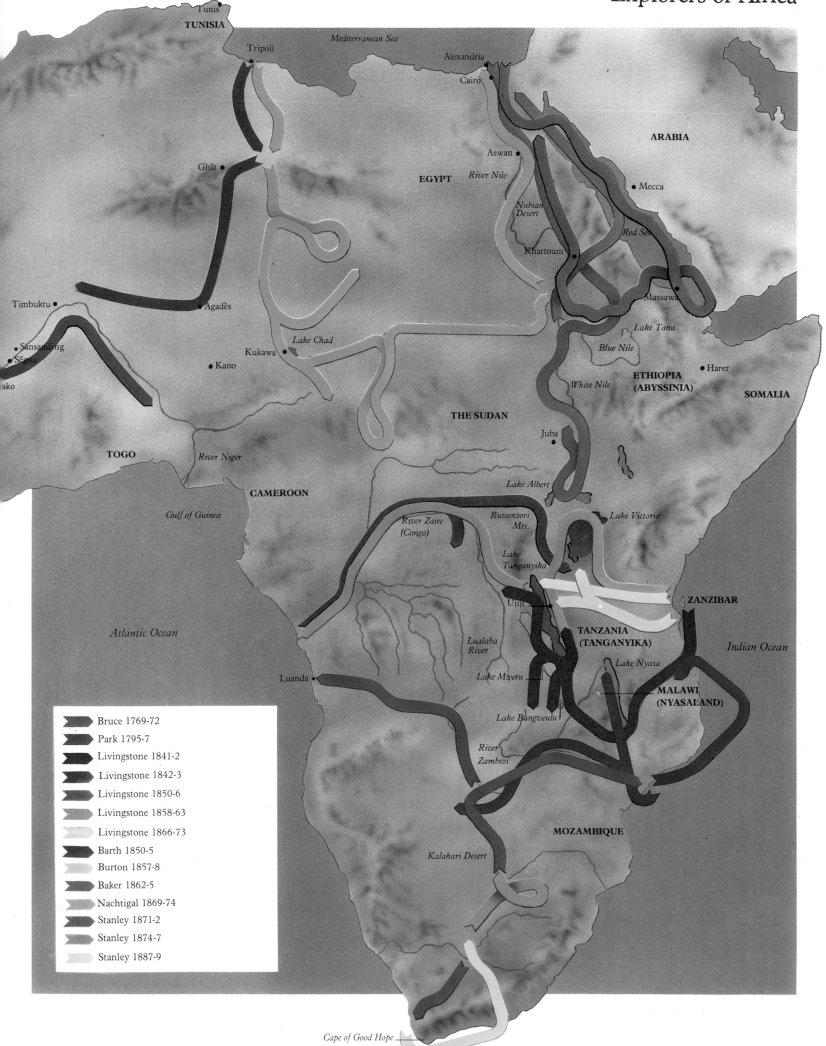

Explorers of Africa

Legend

- Bruce 1769-72
- Park 1795-7
- Livingstone 1841-2
- Livingstone 1842-3
- Livingstone 1850-6
- Livingstone 1858-63
- Livingstone 1866-73
- Barth 1850-5
- Burton 1857-8
- Baker 1862-5
- Nachtigal 1869-74
- Stanley 1871-2
- Stanley 1874-7
- Stanley 1887-9

Place labels:

Tunis, TUNISIA, Tripoli, *Mediterranean Sea*, Alexandria, Cairo, ARABIA, Ghät, Aswan, EGYPT, *River Nile*, Mecca, *Nubian Desert*, *Red Sea*, Timbuktu, Agadès, Khartoum, Massawa, Sansanding, Ségou, Kukawa, *Lake Chad*, Kano, *Lake Tana*, *Blue Nile*, Harer, ETHIOPIA (ABYSSINIA), SOMALIA, *White Nile*, THE SUDAN, Juba, TOGO, *River Niger*, CAMEROON, *Lake Albert*, *Gulf of Guinea*, *River Zaire (Congo)*, *Ruwenzori Mts.*, *Lake Victoria*, *Lake Tanganyika*, Ujiji, ZANZIBAR, TANZANIA (TANGANYIKA), *Indian Ocean*, *Atlantic Ocean*, *Lualaba River*, *Lake Nyasa*, *Lake Mweru*, MALAWI (NYASALAND), Luanda, *Lake Bangweulu*, *River Zambezi*, MOZAMBIQUE, *Kalahari Desert*, *Cape of Good Hope*

James Bruce
(1730–94)

The coastline of Africa had been explored and charted by Portuguese navigators in the fifteenth and sixteenth centuries, but until the eighteenth century the interior remained a fearsome mystery to Europeans. It was known that somewhere in the north-east of the continent, to the west of the Red Sea, lay the source of the great Nile River, which meanders its way across the Nubian Desert to its twenty-mile-wide delta.

James Bruce, laird of Kinnaird, was one of the first Europeans to reach the source of the Blue Nile and trace it to where it joins the White Nile to become the greatest river in Africa. He was a tall, red-haired Scot, good-looking and self-assured, with an ability to adapt to outlandish conditions and a natural fluency in languages.

Having prepared himself by learning Portuguese, Spanish and Arabic, Bruce arrived in Alexandria in 1768, with his Italian secretary Luigi Balugani, determined to find the source of the Nile. He journeyed up it as far as Aswan, where hostile tribesmen forced him to cross the desert and the Red Sea to Jeddah, in Arabia; then, in September 1769, he sailed back across the Red Sea to Massawa. He travelled on towards Gondar, capital of Abyssinia, and was courteously received by the king, Tecla Haimanout, and his vizier,

Above John Smart portrayed Bruce in a white wig, which disguised his own dark red hair. As laird of Kinnaird he was a substantial landowner. It was all the more galling for him, therefore, when his travel stories were widely disbelieved, earning him the nickname 'Macfable'.

Opposite Lake Tana in Ethiopia is the collecting basin of the Blue Nile. Bruce traced the source of the river to Geesh, to a series of little holes in the ground – and was mightily pleased with himself for doing so.

Above Castles built by the Portuguese at Gondar for kings such as Lyasu and Fasil are tourist attractions for modern Ethiopia. Legend said that King Fasil was so covered in hair that he had to kill any concubine who spent the night with him for fear of being exposed as a natural son of the devil.

the extremely cruel and powerful Ras Michael of Tigré.

To his prestige as a traveller from afar Bruce added a slight knowledge of medicine; he assured his welcome in Abyssinia by fumigating the royal palace against smallpox with incense and myrrh, and washing the floors down with vinegar and water. He also won favour by disputing points of religion, such as the relative authenticity of minor miracles, with the *Iteghe* (Queen Dowager).

Bruce described his visit to the court in his *Travels to Discover the Source of the Nile*, written on his return to Scotland. The stories he tells are so fantastic that at the time they were greeted with more amusement than respect. His book was ridiculed and reviled; he was nick-named 'MacFable', and likened to Baron Munchausen, the biggest liar in con-temporary fiction. Although his account of his visit to the court seemed plausible enough to his English readers, one parti-cular incident, on the road near Axum, was greeted with howls of derision. 'Not long after losing sight of the ruins of this ancient capital of Abyssinia we overtook three travellers driving a cow before them,' he began. 'The drivers suddenly tripped up the cow, and gave the animal a very rude fall upon the ground, which was but the beginnings of her sufferings.' One, who had a knife in his hand, 'instead of taking her by the throat . . . gave her a very deep wound in the upper part of her buttock. . . . I let my people go forward and staid myself, till I saw, with the utmost astonishment, two pieces, thicker and longer than our or-dinary beef steaks, cut out of the higher part of the buttock of the beast.' The flap left by the incision was quickly 'fastened to the corresponding part by two or more small skewers, or pins'; the wound was then covered with clay and the animal was allowed to get to her feet. After they had dined on the raw meat, the three men drove the cow off down the road, 'to furnish them with a fuller meal when they should meet their companions in the evening'.

On his second visit to Gondar, Bruce attended an Ethiopian feast. A large cow was brought in and tethered securely in the middle of the hall. Steaks were then cut from its living flesh. 'The prodigious noise the animal makes is a signal for the company to sit down to table,' wrote Bruce. 'The women cut the strips of meat lengthways like strings, dice them and offer them to the men – no man in Abyssinia, in any fashion whatever, feeds himself, or touches his own meat – and all this time the unfortunate victim at the door is bleeding indeed, but bleeding little.' Such banquets were not supposed to be complete without love-making:

The two men nearest the vacuum a pair have made on the bench by leaving their seats, hold their upper garments like a screen before the two that have left the bench. ... Replaced in their seats again, the company drink the happy couple's health; and their example is followed at different ends of the table, as each couple is disposed. All this passes without remark of scandal, not a licentious word is uttered, nor the most distant joke upon the transaction.

Between these visits, in November 1770,

Above The Tissisat Falls on the Blue Nile.

James Bruce

Bruce made his most important discovery: with a troop of imperial horses given to him by Prince Michael, he struck up into the mountains above Gondar, reaching the source of the Blue Nile as it leaves Lake Tana, 6000 feet up. When he told of his reaching the 'fountains of the Nile' this account, too, was scorned. Bruce described how he had been guided to the spot (at the price of a crimson silk sash) by his companion, Wollo; and how he ran 200 yards downhill, throwing off his shoes, hopping over the tangled roots of flowers, to 'the island of green turf, which was in form of an altar'. There he felt impelled to expatiate on the glory of 'standing in that spot which had baffled the genius, industry and enquiry, of both ancients and moderns, for the course of near three thousand years'. The water, 'perfectly pure and limpid', emerged from several springs and seeped through the swamp to a tiny brook. In a cup made of half a coconut shell, Bruce drank a toast to 'King George III and a long line of princes' in clear, cold water.

Next June he said goodbye to the *Iteghe*. One of the chief priests of Gondar, Tensa Christos, asked him to say whether he were 'Frank, Catholic or Jesuit'. Yagoube (the name by which Bruce was commonly known) showed he was Protestant by declaring, 'every man in our country is allowed to serve God in his own way'. Before discussion grew too warm he asked Tensa Christos to forgive him for past offences and bless his journey. 'Is it possible, Yagoube, that you believe my prayers can do you any good?' asked the priest, with tears in his eyes.

After returning to Gondar Bruce followed the Blue Nile down to its confluence with the White Nile at Khartoum. The White Nile, he noticed, was deeper, but nevertheless he mistakenly believed that the Blue Nile was the major river.

Back in London in 1774 he was eager for the fame he felt he deserved. Nobody believed that he had found the source of the Blue Nile, and it was seventeen years before his book found a publisher. In 1792 appeared *A Sequel to the Adventures of Baron Munchausen*, 'humbly dedicated to Mr Bruce, the Abyssinian traveller, as the Baron conceives that it may be some service to him, previous to his making another journey into Abyssinia'; and perhaps the unkindest criticism came from Samuel Johnson, who had himself written a book about Abyssinia, *Rasselas*, without ever going there: his damning verdict was, 'he is not a distinct relater'. It would be many years before almost everything Bruce had written found substantial confirmation in the writings of others.

Below Unlike the White Nile, which meanders much of its way through swamps, the Blue Nile cuts through the hills of Ethiopia to join the White Nile at Khartoum.

Mungo Park
(1771–1806)

In 1778 the Association for Promoting the Discovery of the Interior Parts of Africa was established in Soho Square, London, its aims being to find the River Niger in West Africa and the city of Timbuktu, both of which had first been discovered by Ibn Battūta in the fourteenth century. In 1795 a young doctor, Mungo Park, was instructed by the Association to reach the Niger via the Gambia, to travel to its source via Timbuktu and to return by the same or any other route. He would follow in the steps of two other explorers sent by the Association, both of whom had died in the course of their search.

Park was a typical Scot of the intellectual kind, prudent, diligent and middle class. He was the seventh child of a tenant-farmer's family of thirteen (of which only eight grew up). Whilst studying medicine he became an ardent botanist, and later managed to secure a meeting with Sir Joseph Banks, president of the Royal Society. Anyone supported by Banks – who helped numerous deserving young men – was given a chance of greatness. Mungo was no exception. After a journey to the East Indies as assistant surgeon on the *Worcester*, he was taken on by the newly formed African Association.

After various delays Park found himself on the way to the Gambia on the brig *Endeavour*, a vessel trading in beeswax and ivory, with a letter of credit for £200 (about £4000 today) and a note of recommendation to a Doctor Laidley.

He arrived at Pisania in June 1795 and almost immediately fell ill of a fever. That coast had already acquired a reputation for killing off Europeans. Park spent his convalescence studying the Mandingo language and meeting some *slatees*, the black merchants, 'who came with slaves for the European market'. He left Pisania on 2 December with a negro interpreter called Johnson, a young slave, Demba, lent to him by the doctor, and some slave merchants, who joined him with the intention of journeying with him as long as it might suit. Park took with him as little as possible: a minimum of food, guns and goods for currency, and only a thermometer, compass and pocket sextant for scientific instruments. They travelled north-east towards Senegal, then across to Fatteconda, capital of Bondou, where the king's harem teased Park about his white skin and prominent nose. He travelled on to Teesee and Kooniakary where he met the *slatee* of Soolo, upon whom he had an order 'for the value of five slaves' from Doctor Laidley, and at Kemmoo he met a king with the refreshing name of Daisy Koorabarri who treated him well. When they reached Jarra his servant Johnson, who had conceived a terror of 'the Moors', refused to carry on and had to be sent back with dispatches to the Gambia; but Demba remained faithful.

Previous page A papyrus boat on the Niger river at Mali. Park preferred his own *Joliba*, made from two wooden canoes fastened together, with a shallow draught of no more than a foot. Even in such a boat as that he went aground on a rock at Bussa Rapids and was drowned.

Below right Among many other things Sir Joseph Banks, portly founder of the African Association, was president of the Royal Society. He helped countless young men to greatness. Sailing with Cook on his first voyage he gave him in Batavia a mascot, a brown pottery rabbit which Cook took with him on his next voyage, imprudently leaving it behind on the voyage that proved to be his last.

Below Mungo Park, the young Scots doctor: a miniature after a painting by Henry Edridge. Medicine led to botany and botany to Sir Joseph Banks; hence Park's first journey of exploration on behalf of the African Association.

He arrived at Benowm under armed guard, on the orders of the powerful Ali. As he had travelled through the various kingdoms their rulers had laid claim to most of his small possessions, and now his fortunes sank even further: 'I was a *stranger*, I was *unprotected*, and I was a *Christian*,' he wrote. 'Each of these circumstances is sufficient to drive every spark of humanity from the heart of a Moor.' They thought he was a spy and held him captive for three months.

At Benowm the Moorish ladies tried to undress him ('the reader will easily judge at my surprise at this unexpected declaration'). Park countered them by selecting the youngest and handsomest for the job of taking a look: 'The ladies enjoyed the jest, and went away, laughing heartily; and the young damsel herself to whom I'd given the preference, (though she did not avail herself of the privilege of inspection) seemed no way displeased at the compliment; for she soon after sent me some meat and milk for my supper.' Here also he was deprived of the 'faithful affectionate' Demba, to whom Ali had taken a fancy – though Ali did agree to sell him his own slave, Daman, and allowed him to keep the faithless Johnson, who had been returned to him after being seized by the Moors.

From Benowm Park fled by night towards Bambarra and Ségou, 700 miles inland. At last he was in Negro territory, where the worst expected of him was parting with locks of his hair (for talismans which would confer on the wearer 'all the knowledge of the white man'). Through the Bambarra villages he trudged until at last, near Ségou, the shout went up among his party, '*Geo affilli!*' ('See the water!'). Mungo recorded: 'Looking forwards I saw with infinite pleasure the great object of my mission; the long-sought-for majestic Niger, glittering to the morning sun, as broad as the Thames at Westminster and flowing slowly to the eastward. I hastened to the brink, and having drank of the water, lifted up my fervent thanks in prayer to the Great Ruler of all things, for having thus far crowned my endeavours with success.'

Accordingly, he continued his journey along the Niger's northern bank to Silla, until the rainy season, illness, and further encounters with robbers made him turn back for the Gambia. He met a Muslim slave merchant at Kamalia who allowed Park to travel with his slave caravan to the

Above Mungo Park owed much to the help of *slatees* – free black merchants who came with slaves for the European market – and *bushreens* – Mohammedan slave-dealers. He never indulged in such traffic himself, but like all other early explorers in Africa he had to rely upon slaves to carry his belongings and attend his person.

coast, at a cost of the value of a prime slave. He sailed for Antigua and the Leeward Islands, reaching England in December 1797, after being away for two years and seven months.

Curiously enough, in spite of his fame (and his book, *Travels in the Interior Districts of Africa*, was a great success) another African journey was not immediately proposed to him. Instead, he went back to being a surgeon in Peebles, which bored him considerably. However, in 1803, having strenuously petitioned Joseph Banks, the African Association and the colonial secretary, he managed again to get a commission for an African journey.

Little did he know what was in store for him in the next two years – of the party of over forty men (thirty of them soldiers in impractical uniforms from the garrison at Goree), only eleven, and those all ill, even reached the Niger at Bamaku.

Their boat, the *Joliba*, cleverly constructed from two canoes and with a shallow draught of no more than a foot, bore the survivors along the river beyond Ségou to Sansandig. The river was in flood, and it was a great achievement that the party of four soldiers (one insane), three slaves, one guide and Park, all weakened by disease, managed to get as far as it did. They sailed a thousand miles south-east down the river, expecting to reach the coast, via the Gambia or the Congo in January. But at the Bussa rapids hostile natives attacked the boat with spears. The *Joliba* ran aground, and Park and the others, rather than be a sitting target, jumped into the water and drowned. One slave alone survived to tell the tale. Most of Park's effects and his journals were lost, but the important discovery that the Niger turned to the south, towards the Gulf of Guinea, survived him.

Below 'A view of Kamalia', an engraving from Park's own sketch for his book *Travels in the Interior Districts of Africa*.

Richard Burton
(1821–90)

Richard Burton

Right Burton in Arab dress would have deceived no one had he not been so fluent in so many foreign languages. His habit of 'going native' in various parts of the world earned him uncomplimentary nicknames amongst his disapproving colleagues.

Previous page Burton thought that Lake Tanganyika was the main collecting-basin for the waters of the White Nile. He was wrong.

Right In youth Isabel Arundell was a determined girl who knew what she wanted – Richard Burton. This portrait (by F. Grenfell Baker) shows her in 1890 – the year that she read and destroyed volume after volume of her dead husband's writings.

'I used to like to sit and look at him,' wrote Isabel Arundell, 'and think, "*you are mine, and there is no man on earth the least like you*".' That was as far as the future Lady Burton got with her autobiography. She had 'known' that Richard would be hers long before she met him. The gypsy Hagar Burton had warned her: '*You will cross the sea and be in the same town with your Destiny and know it not. . . . You will bear the name of our tribe and be right proud of it. . . . Your life is all wandering, change and adventure. One soul in two bodies in life or death, never long apart*' – a thrilling fate for a plainish, determined girl, brimful of romantic ideas but without much of a fortune behind her. In her mind's eye she saw him, tall and masterful with 'those strange eyes you dare not take yours off from them'. But when he did not appear in the flesh she feared the

only alternative would be a nunnery. At last, when with her sister on the ramparts of Boulogne, the vision, Richard Burton, in a short black shaggy coat strolled past her. 'That man will marry me!' breathed Isabel. And so he did, eventually.

Meanwhile, Richard Burton had other projects on his mind. He was then twenty-eight and had already survived an extraordinary career in India. Instead of being a run-of-the-mill officer in the Bombay Native Infantry he immersed himself in the study of language and dialect for which he had a flair (he eventually spoke twenty-nine languages and eleven dialects). He became regimental interpreter and much more. Sir Charles Napier, the commander-in-chief, was so impressed by his talents that he employed him as a spy for a top-secret project which was to investigate, heavily disguised, male brothels in Karachi patronized by some of the British troops. By 1847 the findings of so juicily scandalous an enquiry had been fairly thoroughly leaked. Burton became known as 'Dirty Dick' and was accused of freely indulging in the vices he described in his report. One thing, however, *was* clear from the survey – such antics had fascinated the investigator and would do so for the rest of his life.

When he met Isabel, Burton was in the middle of writing more respectably about Sind and its customs. Unaware of her heartfelt sighs he was busy with the idea of making a pilgrimage to Mecca, for which he obtained a year's leave of absence. He duly left England in 1853 disguised as Mirza Abdullah, a Pathan doctor; and was duly the first Englishman to complete the *hadj*.

The fuss made about a pilgrimage enjoined upon *all* Muslims physically able to manage it seems nowadays incredible. Indeed the only thing that made it daring was the fact that Burton was not a Muslim (nor was his European predecessor in Mecca, the Swiss traveller Burkhardt) and so risked being set upon, or killed, if found out.

His exploits made him famous and his books sold well. But when he rejoined his regiment in Bombay the notorious young officer soon aroused intense jealousy. He worked hard to get further leave for another expedition, this time to Harer, in Somalia, the largest slave-market in East Africa; for this the Royal Geographical Society was prepared to put up £1000.

The expedition was to have consisted of Lieutenant Herne, Lieutenant Stroyan and another man; but this man died and accordingly, John Speke, a young Indian Army officer, mad on shooting, got his chance of joining. Burton insisted on riding into Harer without his companions, staying there, in danger of his life, for ten days, and riding back to Aden alone across the desert, almost without provisions. Meanwhile, Speke had been detailed to explore the Wadi Nogal. When they met again in Aden, the tall, good-looking Speke had failed even to find Wadi Nogal, but had shot quantities of game. Burton's scorn met Speke's bewildered tendency to bluff it out, and from then on there was a lasting tension between them. Their subsequent expedition into Somalia was a disastrous failure – natives attacked their party, killing one member, and wounding Burton and Speke.

Below 'Grandee's Litter'. The pilgrimage to Mecca enjoined upon all Muslims physically capable of the effort was performed by Burton in disguise. Others were carried along in grand style. All equally would have to trudge on foot round the *Kaaba*, the Muslim Holy of Holies containing a sacred black meteorite.

Above Apart from Isabel, his wife, who was clearly a special case, Burton showed little enthusiasm for the ladies, even such as the pretty Bedouin girls who went about largely without the veil which so many Muslim women had to wear.

In 1857 Burton made his most important expedition, to discover the source of the White Nile. Incomplete exploration of East Africa had led to the idea that inland lay a huge lake, as big as the Caspian Sea; Burton proposed an expedition to determine the actual size of this lake (which turned out in fact to be a combination of Lakes Tanganyika, Victoria and Nyasa). His instructions from the Royal Geographical Society were

to penetrate inland from Kilwa . . . on the east coast of Africa and make the best of your way to the reputed Lake Nyasa. . . . Having obtained all the information you require in this quarter you are to proceed northwards towards the range of mountains marked on our maps as containing the probable source of the Nile, which it will be your next great object to discover.

Surprisingly, Burton asked for Speke to accompany him.

With a 130 porters, thirty donkeys and provisions for two years they set off from Zanzibar, following the Arab caravan route into the interior. Five months later, 900 miles from their starting point, they reached Lake Tanganyika, 2500 feet up in the Great Rift Valley. Burton was so ill with malaria he could hardly walk and Speke was partly blind, but the exhausted men could not fail to respond to the magnificence of the vast lake, the second largest in Africa, surrounded by towering peaks. Burton wrote:

Nothing could be more picturesque than this first view of the Tanganyika Lake, as it lay in the lap of the mountains, basking in the gorgeous tropical sunshine. The shores of this vast crevasse appeared doubly beautiful to me after the silent and spectral mangrove-creeks of East African seaboard, and the melancholy, monotonous experience of desert and jungle scenery, tawny rock and sun-parched plain or rank herbage and flats of black mire. . . .

Too ill to continue, they returned from Ujiji to Tabora. Speke recovered first and set off northwards across boulder-strewn plains. 200 miles away he discovered the lake he named Victoria, after the queen. This, despite Burton's conviction that Lake Tanganyika was the Nile's collecting basin, Speke was convinced was the true source of the Nile:

I no longer felt any doubt that the lake at my feet gave birth to that interesting river, the source of which had been the subject of so much speculation, and the object of so many explorers.

Each man hotly defended his own theory, and they parted in Aden on the

Above Navigation of the Tanganyika Lake: a plate from Burton's own book. Though crippled and half blinded with malaria, Burton could not fail to be moved by the beauty of the lake.

Opposite Strange things grow in Unyamwesi, 'Land of the Moon': a plate from Burton's book *The Lake Regions of Central Africa.*

worst possible terms. Burton made the mistake of staying behind and letting Speke reach London two weeks ahead of him. The inevitable happened: Speke claimed the lion's share of the credit.

The row which followed was prolonged and bitter. It was made worse when Speke and James Grant alone were chosen for the next Nile expedition. Matters came to a head in 1864 when Sir Roderick Murchison arranged a debate between Burton and Speke, at a meeting of the British Association for the Advancement of Science, with Livingstone in the chair. Speke was expected to defend his theory that Lake Victoria was the true source of the Nile. The day before, Speke was found shot dead, apparently having committed suicide.

By then Isabel had married Richard and had tasted the delights and disadvantages of having someone so hypnotic for a husband. Richard was rather too much of a nomad for her liking; he was in Fernando Po and she was not. But from then on she often managed to travel with him, in Portugal and in Brazil, which was less tame, and where Richard had found a niche in the British Consular Service. At São Paolo, after a lone excursion in a canoe, he nearly died: his 'Zookins' (his pet name for her) nursed him devotedly, with all the intensity of one dedicated to a cause, and he recovered. After that, her life was transformed. With him she went to Palmyra and

Damascus; finally they settled in Trieste. News of a knighthood, with which the British government had decided to honour him, reached him in Tangier.

General Gordon tried to lure him to the Sudan, but he would have none of it: he wanted to devote himself to writing. Following his *Arabian Nights Entertainments*, a *succès de scandale* at last, he was busy with *The Perfumed Garden*. Nothing he had learned in Sind or elsewhere had been forgotten. His works were annotated in great detail, and contained daring essays on homosexuality and pornography. 'I have put my whole life and all my life-blood into that [*The Perfumed Garden*]. It is my great hope that I shall live by it. It is the crown of my life,' he told his doctor. Over one thousand pages long, it was just about finished when, in October 1890, having signed a statement that he had genuinely joined the Roman Catholic Church (to make Isabel happy), Burton died.

Isabel spent the next sixteen days reading through every word of his notes and diaries. Then, she wrote, 'sorrowfully, reverently, and in fear and trembling, I burnt sheet after sheet, until the whole of the volumes were consumed'. Thus she destroyed everything she had found shocking during their life together. But like a phoenix Richard Burton's reputation rose indestructible from the ashes and has been in the ascendant ever since.

Samuel and Florence Baker
(1821–93)   (c1842–1916)

The nineteenth century was a great time for African exploration. Four years after Burton and Speke had discovered Lakes Tanganyika and Victoria, in 1861 Samuel and Florence Baker started their first journey in Central and East Africa to discover the sources of the Nile.

The expedition would combine this search and a rendezvous with the government-sponsored Speke-Grant expedition which had set off from Zanzibar to follow up the controversial Burton-Speke expedition. It was also to be a shooting safari: Baker was a Victorian gentleman of a very different breed from the scholarly and sardonic Richard Burton. He was a sportsman, the author of *Rifle and Hound in Ceylon*, and to him exploration was the greatest of sports. He also believed in comfort: he would scout danger with equanimity sustained by a hamper of good things from Fortnum and Mason, while his Hungarian-born wife, who accompanied him on his arduous travels, cheerfully faced the rigours of camping with the help of a luxuriously fitted portable dressing table.

He was always a successful man and he was never far removed from his sport. He had founded a plantation in Ceylon, and built a railway to connect the Danube to the Black Sea. With one family already behind him, he turned to exploration with his

Above Sir Samuel Baker was primarily interested in bagging animals, and wrote a book, *Rifle and Hound in Ceylon*, to prove it. A jolly man, with an immense beard, he had the good sense to marry Florence, a Hungarian woman who enjoyed going on safari provided that she could do it in style.

Opposite The White Nile cascading from Lake Victoria into the lake the Bakers christened 'Lake Albert'.

second wife, Florence. Her calm amid the dangers they encountered must have been invaluable to him: 'Mrs Baker was not a screamer,' he explained, 'and never even whispered: in the moment of suspected danger, a touch of my sleeve was considered a sufficient warning.'

In December 1862 the Bakers left Khartoum to travel up the Nile by boat. Two months later they were at Gondokoro, where they met Speke and Grant, weary from their travels. Baker, with his immense spade beard, greeted them heartily, but Speke and Grant brought both welcome and unwelcome news. They had established Lake Victoria as one (but not the only) main collecting basin of the Nile. The river ran out of it at the north end, over the Ripon Falls. 'Is there not one leaf of the laurel left for me?' asked Baker anxiously. The reply was encouraging: the two explorers told them that there was supposed to be another lake to the northwest of Lake Victoria into which the Nile flowed before flowing out again, but the difficult and obstructive Kamrasi, king of Unyoro, had made it impossible for them to attempt to find it.

Thanking Speke and Grant for their 'characteristic candour and generosity' in pointing out where this lake was supposed to be on the map, the Bakers set off in some style on an expedition to find Kamrasi. In the event, when they found the king, after months of rough travelling, they mistook (as they were intended to do) his brother M'gambi for him. Their porters had deserted and M'gambi supplied more men, but only after grabbing a multitude of presents, including Mrs Baker's muslin scarf, the last she had; and finally he demanded that the lady herself should be left behind for his pleasure. Baker drew himself up, revolver at the ready. Florence, 'naturally indignant, had risen from her seat; and maddened with the excitement of the moment, she made him a little speech in Arabic (not a word of which he understood), with a countenance almost as amiable as the head of Medusa'. Flabbergasted, M'gambi protested that he had intended no offence and provided them with an escort of 300 men for the last leg of their journey to the greak lake to the northwest of Speke's Lake Victoria.

On the journey all but thirteen of the

Below In the Victorian tradition of tales of adventure, every picture tells a story. Compared with her husband's sensible garb, Florence seems over-dressed. Doubtless she valued the aura of respectability above comfort.

brigade (called by Baker 'The Devil's own') had to be sent back. Then Florence fell ill: on turning round to beckon to her, Samuel was 'horrified to see her standing on one spot, and sinking gradually through the weeds, while her face was distorted and perfectly purple'. To his utmost alarm, 'she fell, as though shot dead. . . . It was a *coup de soleil*!' Insensible in a litter, she was carried along for a week in a sunstroke coma, followed by convulsions. They had stopped in a village and were already looking for some suitable place in which to bury her when she sat up and started recovering.

The march was resumed and the lake, loyally christened 'Lake Albert', was reached on 14 March 1864: 'The boundless sheet of water lay like a mirror. . . .' The Bakers tottered, arm-in-arm, towards a white and pebbly beach. Leaving Florence, Samuel went to the water's edge, drank a long draught and later he wrote:

It is impossible to describe the triumph of that moment – here was the reward for all our labour – for all the years of tenacity with which we had toiled through Africa. England had won the sources of the Nile!

In fact the real source of the Nile is far to the south of Lake Albert, in the Ruwenzori Highlands, but gradually the mystery of the Nile's course was being solved. From the great basin of Lake Victoria the river flowed out over the Ripon Falls (now part of the Owen Falls dam named after the pioneer in Uganda, Roddy Owen) to the steep, dramatic Murchison falls, teeming with crocodiles, (which the Bakers named after Sir Roderick Murchison, president of

the Royal Geographical Society), where it emptied itself into Lake Albert before proceeding on its way towards Wadelai; thence, interrupted by rapids, it flowed to Gondokoro and down to the cataracts of Sudan and Egypt. It only remained to discover where the contents of the two lakes came from.

After two and a half years' travelling they reached Khartoum, and then returned to England, where honours and acclaim awaited them: gold medals from the Royal Geographical Society and its counterpart

Above Baker's watercolour sketch of the 'Kamrasi escort'. M'gambi, King Kamrasi's brother – who, to confuse matters, was posing as Kamrasi – provided the Bakers with an escort of three hundred men they called 'The Devil's own': all but thirteen had to be sent back to their real master during the journey to Lake Albert.

Below Sir Samuel's own view of himself and Florence in a native village.

Above Samuel Baker 'Overhauling the Giraffe' between Obbo and Latooka: his own watercolour from his Lake Albert expedition of 1863.

Below At Murchison Falls the Victoria Nile bursts through so small a gorge into Lake Albert that Winston Churchill, who was there as a young man, wrote: 'I doubt whether it is fifteen feet across from sheer rock to sheer rock.'

in Paris: a knighthood followed in 1865 for 'services rendered to geographical science'. Baker wrote successful books about his travels, and on that note his life might have resumed the more even tenor of a sporting Victorian gentleman's existence. But another visit to Egypt for the opening of the Suez Canal in 1869 changed the course of his life.

The Khedive Ismail, who was bankrupting himself mounting glittering entertainments for his guests, among them the Empress Eugénie and the Prince and Princess of Wales, asked Baker to accept an appointment as Governor-General of the equatorial Nile basin, and to take command of an expedition for the suppression of the slave trade on the White Nile and the establishment of order in the Sudan. Baker accepted the appointment: 'All is signed, sealed and delivered; and I have the most absolute power over the southern Nile basin.'

The appointment proved to be a crown of thorns, since its two objects were incompatible; the slave traders and their organizations alone held the key to public order. Tentacles of bribery reached out to every official who had even the slightest control. At Unyoro, Baker quashed a revolt, greatly assisted by the calm behaviour of his wife. At Fatiko he won a skirmish against some slavers; but as his biographers Murray and White put it, he came to recognize later that 'measures of forcible repression were all very well for punitive or police purposes; but they did not strike at the root of the mischief' – which was, that few people in Africa, including the khedive, really wanted to get rid of the slave trade, whatever their protestations. When a fighting movement of religious expansionism led by the *mahdi* was added to this equivocal situation, it was small wonder that General Gordon, Baker's successor, was overwhelmed by disaster at Khartoum.

The Bakers were an early example of a husband-and-wife team, the epitome of Victorian empire builders.

David Livingstone (1813–73)
and Henry Morton Stanley (1841–1904)

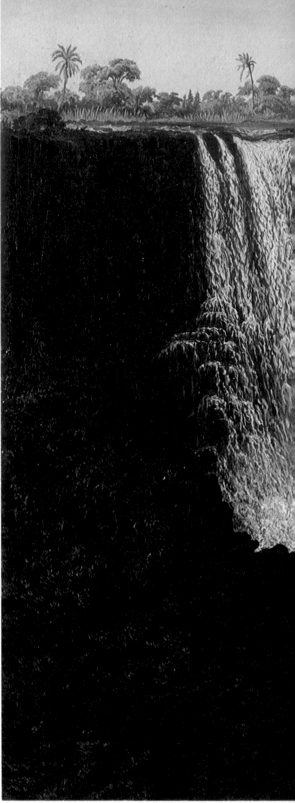

Above Dr Livingstone, the craggy Scot whose early years were spent in a cotton mill. As a missionary he would have originally preferred a posting to China; but when he was sent instead to Africa he never doubted that it was the Lord's will.

Previous page Thomas Baines' painting of Livingstone at the Kebrasa rapids above Teke on the Zambezi.

The further Europeans penetrated into Africa, the more they became concerned for the souls of the Africans they encountered. Mission stations sprang up wherever there was a settlement, and very often missionaries were pioneers into uncharted territories. David Livingstone, one of the greatest of all the explorers of Africa, was also one of the greatest missionaries: it was his missionary zeal that sent him on his first expedition into the bush.

Livingstone was a craggy Scot, largely self-taught during early years spent in a cotton mill. Without hesitation he went to South Africa in 1840 as a missionary, and quickly realized that whilst converting the natives was the proper task, someone had to pioneer the setting up of mission stations by travelling through the wilderness.

Over the next fifteen years Livingstone was constantly pushing northwards across the Kalahari Desert, making many gruelling journeys, often accompanied by his wife and three young children. When his wife gave birth to their fourth child on one of the expeditions, Livingstone realized that his young family needed education and security, and could not endure such hardship; so he sent them back to Scotland.

Now that he was alone, he was free to push himself to the limits of endurance, and made his intention clear: 'I shall open up a path into the interior, or perish.' He planned to find a route, suitable for trade, from the Zambezi to the Atlantic coast, 1800 miles away.

On 11 November 1853 he set off north-westward from Luijanti at the approaches to the Zambezi, with twenty-seven porters, canoes, a tent, food, a few clothes, and scientific instruments. Five and a half months later, on 31 May 1854, he reached the sea at Luanda, half-starved, and weakened with fever and dysentery. He had covered 1500 miles of land never before seen by a European, through rain forests, swamps

and land inhabited by hostile peoples.

Livingstone, however, with his boundless energy and dedication, determined on making the return journey, partly to take his porters back home, and partly because he was dissatisfied with the route he had taken. In September the party set off up the Cuanza River, and a year later reached Luijanti. Livingstone had nearly died of rheumatic fever on the journey, but after only seven weeks was on the move again, this time eastwards along the Zambezi to reach the east coast. In May 1856 he reached Quilimane in Mozambique, having discovered the Victoria Falls on the Zambezi, 'the most wonderful sight I had witnessed in Africa'.

Whenever he could, he sent back accounts of his journeys complete with detailed astronomical and hydrographical observations. His expeditions contradicted one generally held belief: the rivers of Africa, far from petering out into nothing among arid wastes, as in Australia, were great waterways, watering fertile country.

The published account of his travels

Above The Great Western Wall, Victoria Falls, by Thomas Baines.

Above Thomas Baines' painting of the boat *Ma-Robert*, called after the natives' name for Livingstone's wife, aground at the head of the eastern branch of the West Luabo river.

Below Livingstone's house in Tanzania.

quickly became a best-seller, and on his return to England in 1856 he was greeted as a major African explorer. He had moved beyond the field of missionary endeavour and he went back to Africa with the grandiloquent title, 'Her Majesty's consul at Quilimane for the eastern coast and the independent districts of the interior'. He was also to command 'an expedition for exploring eastern and central Africa, for the promotion of commerce and civilization with a view to the extinction of the slave trade'.

From 1858 to 1864 he explored the Zambezi: with a paddle steamer called after the natives' name for his wife, *Ma Robert*, he explored Lake Nyasa; and with the *Lady Nyasa*, built at his own expense, the Ruvuma River. It was on this expedition that he encountered appalling sights: long lines of men, women and children, manacled and being driven to slave markets.

He conceived a greater and greater horror of the slave trade, and returning once more to England, he succeeded in interesting private and public bodies in the idea of 'civilizing influences' to follow exploration in Nyasaland and Tanganyika.

In 1866 he set out, like many explorers before him, to find the source of the Nile. With the title of British consul to Central Africa (unpaid), he disembarked in Zanzibar (he called it 'Stinkibar'), and after much exploration round Lake Mweru, Lake Bangweulu, and the Lualaba River (which he thought was a major Nile tributary) he arrived in Ujiji, teeth falling out, his body racked with malaria – a mere 'ruckle of bones'.

At Nyangwe, on the Lualaba, Livingstone had witnessed a massacre by slavers of hundreds of innocent natives in their own market place; and one day he came upon a party of slaves sitting, singing and laughing:

Hallo! said I, These fellows take to it kindly; this must be the class for whom philosophers say slavery is the natural state. And I went and asked them the cause of their mirth. . . . They were using it to express the idea of haunting, as a ghost, and inflicting disease and death; and the song was, '*Yes, we are going away to Manga* [abroad in white man's land] *with yokes on our necks; but we shall have no yokes in death. And we shall return to haunt and kill you*'.

One of the results of Livingstone's campaign was the suppression by the sultan of Zanzibar of his own profitable slave market.

And then it seemed that the good doctor was lost. No one could get news of him. He was reported killed; then reported alive.

After abortive attempts by others, the first expedition to reach him, in 1871, was headed by the American, Henry Morton Stanley of the *New York Herald*:

In a few minutes we shall have reached the spot where lives, we imagine, the object of our search. . . . The flags are fluttered . . . the banner of America is in front, waving joyfully. . . . The natives of Ujiji . . . hurry up by the hundreds to ask what it all means . . . there are *Yambos* (how-do-you-do's) shouted out to me by the dozen. . . . There are hundreds of people around me – I might say thousands without exaggeration. It seems to me it is a great triumphal procession. There is a group of the most respectable Arabs; and as I come nearer I see the white face of an old man among them. He has a cap with a gold band around it; his dress is a short jacket of red blanket-cloth; and his pants – well, I didn't observe. I am shaking hands with him. We raise our hats, and I say: 'Dr Livingstone, I presume?' And he says: 'Yes.'

Livingstone accompanied Stanley to explore the northern reaches of Lake Tanganyika but, indomitable, refused to return to England with him. Obsessed with the twin need to discover the Nile's source and destroy the slave trade he moved south again. But for his five last years of exploration he had been a sick man, and in 1873 he died at Ulala, worn out with chronic dysentery. His Negro servants buried his entrails in a tin box under a large tree, on which was cut the inscription: 'Doctor Livingstone died on May 4th 1873.' In quasi-biblical language, no doubt absorbed from his close association with such a man,

one of his servants wrote: 'He rode a donkey, but subsequently was carried, and thus arrived at Ulala, beyond Lake Bembe, in Bisa country, when he said: "Build me a hut to die in".'

His body, preserved in salt and dried in the sun, started twelve days later on an amazing journey of nine months to the coast, carried for over a thousand miles through territory of friend and foe alike by a little band of devoted natives. No one has ever really fathomed what magical hopes and fears impelled them. The original bark coffin was prudently exchanged for a smaller one, done up as a bale of cloth to conceal its identity, and in that way reached Zanzibar. As they journeyed, the donkey on which the doctor had ridden for the last time was attacked and killed by a lion. But Livingstone's clothing, instruments and papers survived; and of these the latter proved a potent force for good long after their author's death. His body was buried in Westminster Abbey, with great

Above The famous meeting at Ujiji, 10 November 1871.

Above left H. M. Stanley, star reporter: a foundling from St Asaph's workhouse in Wales, and a very tough man. He recognized the greatness of Dr Livingstone straight away.

Previous page The Congo river basin, Zaire.

ceremony, in April 1874 and *The Last Journals of David Livingstone* were published the same year.

After Livingstone's death, Stanley went on to make his own important contribution to European knowledge of Africa: the discovery and development of the Congo.

Stanley was a Welsh workhouse foundling who ran away to America. He fought on both sides in the American Civil War, first in the Confederate Army, then in the Federal Navy, before journeying through Asia Minor on a shoe-string. On his return he became a newspaperman; his meeting with Livingstone was a scoop for the *New York Herald* which incidentally set him on the road to becoming one of the greatest explorers of Africa. And he did it all on tea: 'I'm like an old woman,' he said, 'I love tea very much, and can take a quart and a half without any inconvenience.'

Sponsored by the *Daily Telegraph*, Stanley set off to solve once and for all the problem of the Nile sources and the size and position of the lakes: neither Baker, Speke, Burton nor Livingstone had managed to solve it, and Stanley himself had always confused the sources of the Nile with those of the Congo River. In 1874 he left Zanzibar for Lake Victoria, which he reached four months later. On the journey many of his party had died of disease or in attacks by marauding tribesmen, and large numbers of his porters had deserted. On the shores of Lake Victoria they assembled the *Lady Alice*, a forty-foot collapsible steel boat, which they had carried in sections from the coast. He circumnavigated the lake, and confirmed Speke's assertion that the Nile did indeed flow from it. Then he turned south to Lake Tanganyika, which he proved not to be the source of the Nile.

Turning eastwards, with enormous difficulty the party reached the confluence of Luana and Lualaba rivers in October 1876. Guided by Tippoo Tib, an Arab slave trader, the men, women and children followed the Lualaba on foot through rain forest so dense that it was as dark as night in the daytime. Worn down with smallpox, dysentery and ulcers, Tippoo Tib's men abandoned Stanley 200 miles north of Nyangwe. The party continued, pursued by cannibals, and with no idea of what lay before them. Where the Lualaba becomes the Congo cataracts forced them to man-handle their boats up cliffs and through the bush. They could not know that they now had a thousand miles of plain sailing to the mouth of the Congo in front of them.

They arrived at the Atlantic, 115 survivors out of 356, on 1 August 1877, two years and nine months after they had set out.

With Stanley's exploration of the Congo the great age of African exploration was over: the Niger, the Zambezi, the Nile and the Congo had been charted, and the number, size and position of the great lakes was known. Now both the coastline and the interior of the continent were known in detail in Europe.

Retired from the African scene, Stanley stood for parliament, and in 1894 was elected member for North Lambeth. In 1899 he was knighted. Five years later he died quietly at his home in Whitehall.

Below At Nyangwe, on the Lualuaba river, Livingstone witnessed a massacre by slaves of hundreds of Africans; a sight which gave him 'a vivid impression of being in Hell'. It was just as bad when slaves were abandoned to die of starvation.

Heinrich Barth (1821–65) and Gustav Nachtigal (1834–85)

In the nineteenth-century stampede by the nations of Europe to plant their national flags all over Africa, a regrouped and vigorous Germany was not likely to lag behind. If others had got in earlier with discoveries and trading posts, then better late than never with explorers – helped by a little judicious diplomacy.

Heinrich Barth was the greatest German explorer of Africa in the 1850s. He was well qualified in history, geography, archaeology and Arabic and his methods were highly scientific. In 1850 he left Tripoli on an expedition sent by the British government to explore the area between Lake Chad and the Niger and to negotiate trade treaties with the rulers of West Sudan. The three members of the expedition, James Richardson, an Englishman, Adolf Overweg, a German geologist, and Barth set off southwards across the Sahara to Ghat. Crossing the Air Mountains they reached Agadès, where they split up, Richardson to go east to Lake Chad, while Barth and Overweg continued westward. Barth disguised himself as a Muslim scholar to visit Kano, a town of about 30,000 people.

When he and Overweg reached Lake Chad, they found that Richardson had died of fever. They negotiated with the sultan of Bornu, the ferocious sultanate which lay on the southern edge of the Sahara, now in northern Nigeria, whom they found to be interested in trade but not in abolishing slavery, and spent fifteen months exploring the rivers and lands around Lake Chad.

In 1852 Overweg died of malaria, and Barth set off on the long trek westward to Timbuktu. He arrived there ten months later, in September 1853, and stayed there for eight months before returning to Kukawa. South of Lake Chad he was joined by Vogel, another German explorer, and as ill-fated as Barth's other companions: he was murdered.

When Barth eventually left Kukawa, in May 1855, he had made one of the most fruitful and remarkable series of journeys ever undertaken in inner Africa. The length of his stays in the places he visited is evidence of his unusual ability to get on with his African hosts, and his scholarly training encouraged him to make minute studies of the resources, history, topography and customs of their countries. He was an early example of an explorer with a broadly anthropological, rather than colonial, attitude to the peoples he encountered.

In the interests of diplomacy, it was felt that the tolerance shown to German visitors by

Above Heinrich Barth, a man well qualified in history, geography, archaeology and Arabic, and a traveller in advance of his times.

Opposite A contemporary lithograph by G. F. Lyon of 'A Sand Wind on the Desert.' Sandstorms are still dreaded in the desert; there is nothing to be done except to lie low and wait for them to blow over.

Top and above Taken from original sketches by Barth, these lithographs of a native village and the interior of a dwelling indicate his anthropological interest in the peoples he met.

the sultan of Bornu should be reciprocated with a gesture of thanks from the king of Prussia. Bornu had first been entered in 1823 by British explorers, who had reported seeing Negro knights 'habited in coats of mail composed of iron chain, which covered them from throat to knees', and since then its people had had a reputation for great ferocity. Vogel, who had gone to look for Barth, had himself vanished, and it was with relief at Barth's safe return in 1855 that the king decided to make this flattering gesture. Suggesting equality, as from one powerful ruler to another, the king was pleased to send an emissary bearing gifts to Sheikh Omar, 'to thank him for assistance given to German travellers passing through his land'.

Gustav Nachtigal was his emissary. Originally an army surgeon, son of a Lutheran pastor, he had always sighed for warmer climes and had been particularly attracted to the Arab world. Satisfying both those wishes by becoming physician to the Bey of Tunis, he had made use of the opportunity to study Arabic and Arabic customs in order to be able to travel amongst Arabs 'as one of them'.

Heinrich Barth and Gustav Nachtigal

As the king's emissary, he duly set out for Tripoli in 1868 bearing a strange load of assorted gifts: a silver tea service, some special rose essences, silks and satins, an obligatory portrait of the king, even an ornate portable harmonium. Exploring the Tibesti Massif en route, Nachtigal arrived in Kukawa (he always called it Kuka), Bornu's capital, to be welcomed by women on their knees waving ostrich-feather fans and other exotic delights. He described in detail the brilliant escort of the heir-presumptive, including 'a band of musicians, as numerous as they were discordant, with gold and silver *burnoos*' and multicoloured pantaloons. The heavy cavalry was still caparisoned like a survival from the Middle Ages. But he saw little of Kukawa: strangers and Arabs were put up in a separate, western cantonment, away from the sultan's huge family of hangers-on in the eastern city; in addition it poured with rain and local custom, he observed, 'prevents a man going out on foot'.

The presents were a success. The portable harmonium, wheezing from a

Left Gustav Nachtigal: the king's emissary to the Sultan of Bornu and later Germany's imperial commissioner to Africa. His skilful treaty arrangements added Togoland and Cameroon to the German empire.

Below A lithograph from Barth's sketch of a Karemma Chief, suggesting power as well as splendour.

combination of excessive heat and damp, gave trouble; but it soon yielded to the skilled attentions of Valpreda, an Italian engineer Nachtigal had brought with him.

Nachtigal could now continue his journey through the desert areas to the east. Disguised as a Muslim pilgrim, he travelled through Wadai and across the Sudan to Darfur and Kordofan. Wadai was particularly dangerous for travellers: he learnt why Vogel had been murdered there some years earlier: religious fanatics had decided that his pencil was a magic wand, and therefore dangerous.

Nachtigal reached Cairo in November 1874, and soon began work on an excellent account of his travels. His success put him in line for political promotion. When France induced Tunisia to become a protectorate, Nachtigal was made German consul-general, and in 1884 he was sent to West Africa as imperial commissioner.

Nachtigal was to get what he could for Germany; and by then there was not much left between the Gambia and the Niger. However, Togoland was still unclaimed: a narrow strip of coast, swamps and lagoons, extending backwards into healthier hill country. Merchants from Bremen had long established themselves there, and, using their establishments as his base, Nachtigal arranged for the king of Togo to put himself under German suzerainty on 5 July 1884. In the Cameroons, the much larger territory stretching from the coast nearly as far as Lake Chad, Nachtigal concluded a treaty with the picturesquely named King Bell on 15 July. He thus forestalled a British mission with a similar purpose arriving five days later, and a French mission (supported by a gun-boat) which arrived six days after that. The victorious Allies confiscated both colonies from Germany after the First World War, but in the thirties Hitler included in a portfolio of territorial ambitions 'the return of the colonies of Togoland and Kamerun'.

Nachtigal's return should have been triumphant. To have travelled so far, so effectively, to have loved the Arabs so knowledgeably, and finally to have added so much to the imperial greatness of his country merited great rewards. But in 1885 he died at sea, before reaching Germany.

The Polar Regions

Commerce first prompted an interest in Arctic exploration, as men searched for a North-west Passage between Europe and Cathay. However, as other ways of getting there were gradually discovered, the search became less urgent, and moreover, as North America and Canada and the semi-frozen seas and islands began to take shape on the charts following the efforts of Davis, Hudson, Barents, Frobisher, Fox and Parry, it became clear that the North-west Passage was not only difficult but commercially useless – a verdict which is still valid today. In 1969 the giant supertanker, *Manhattan*, helped by satellite tracking stations and every technological device available, went crushing through the ice of a passage found by MacClure to see if this or any other North-west Passage could be a viable alternative route to the Alaskan oilfields. The voyage confirmed that the route was possible but scarcely profitable.

The race to reach the North Pole attracted much public interest. Nansen in the *Fram*, adrift in the ice, hoped to be carried across it. Peary and Cook crossed the ice with sledges and dogs to reach it, and then squabbled about who had got there first. In 1926 Commander Byrd flew over it, and in 1958 an American nuclear-powered submarine, *Nautilus*, glided under it; in 1976 the crew of HMS *Sovereign* surfaced near it for a game of football in temperatures of $-35°$ Centigrade ($-31°$ Fahrenheit).

There was less reason to explore the Antarctic. No routes lay through it, and there were no scattered islands in semi-frozen seas. Nevertheless international curiosity was aroused. After Cook's voyage of discovery, a Russian expedition under Bellinghausen nosed at the great land mass and its pack-ice in 1819. The French under d'Urville were also active, as was Lieutenant Wilkes of the US Navy. After that, James Clark Ross, whose job (following Humboldt's representations to the British Government) was to set up magnetic stations, was the first considerable Antarctic explorer. He was to make another name for himself in the Arctic, actually reaching the North Magnetic Pole on foot, to find nothing more dramatic than some abandoned Eskimo huts.

The Norwegian flag was planted at the South Pole, so nearly reached by Shackleton, by the ubiquitous Amundsen. There unfolded one of the great epics of all time, the tragic story of the expedition led by Captain Scott, the epitome of the carefully trained but still, somehow, amateur explorer, and of the unselfish behaviour of those men in their last terrible hours.

Amundsen, by far the most ruthless, was the most successful explorer of his era. In the Arctic he was the first to sail all the way through a North-west Passage (others had done it differently, and partly on foot). In the Antarctic he was first to reach the Pole. His death, in search of Nobile, was in the heroic tradition. And yet somehow just as the Arctic is linked for ever with the name of Franklin, his expedition a failure, breathing his last on board a ship beset in a frozen sea, so it is the figure of Scott dying in his tent in a blizzard which prevails when we think of the Antarctic.

The American, Richard Byrd, reached the North Pole by air in 1926. Three years later he circled the South Pole before touching down at his base near the Bay of Whales. And now – a fitting tribute to our times – the icy wastes of the South Pole are within easy, if expensive, reach of the tourist with a taste for the uncomfortable. As for the North Pole, today's traveller from Europe to Alaska crosses high above it on a regular, scheduled air service and may not even bother to make it out if the in-flight film is entertaining enough.

Explorers of the Polar Regions

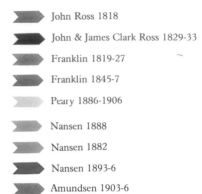

	John Ross 1818
	John & James Clark Ross 1829-33
	Franklin 1819-27
	Franklin 1845-7
	Peary 1886-1906
	Nansen 1888
	Nansen 1882
	Nansen 1893-6
	Amundsen 1903-6

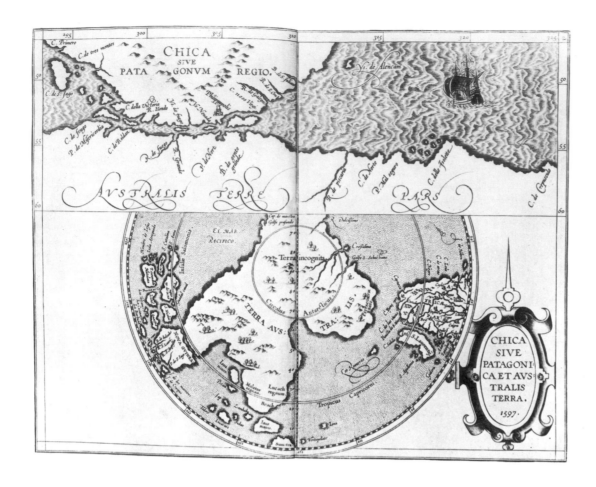

Left A map published in 1597 shows the Antarctic Circle as 'Terra incognita', at the heart of the imaginery southern continent, 'Terra Australis'.

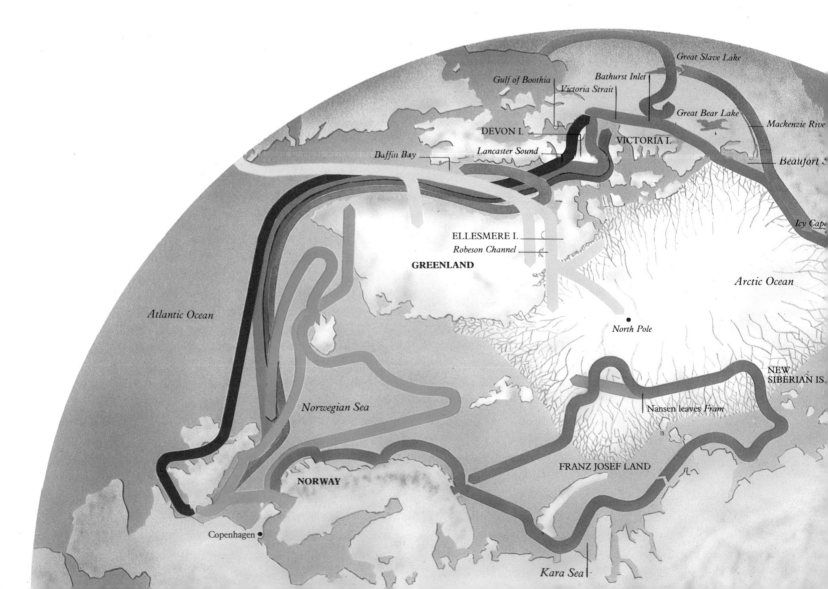

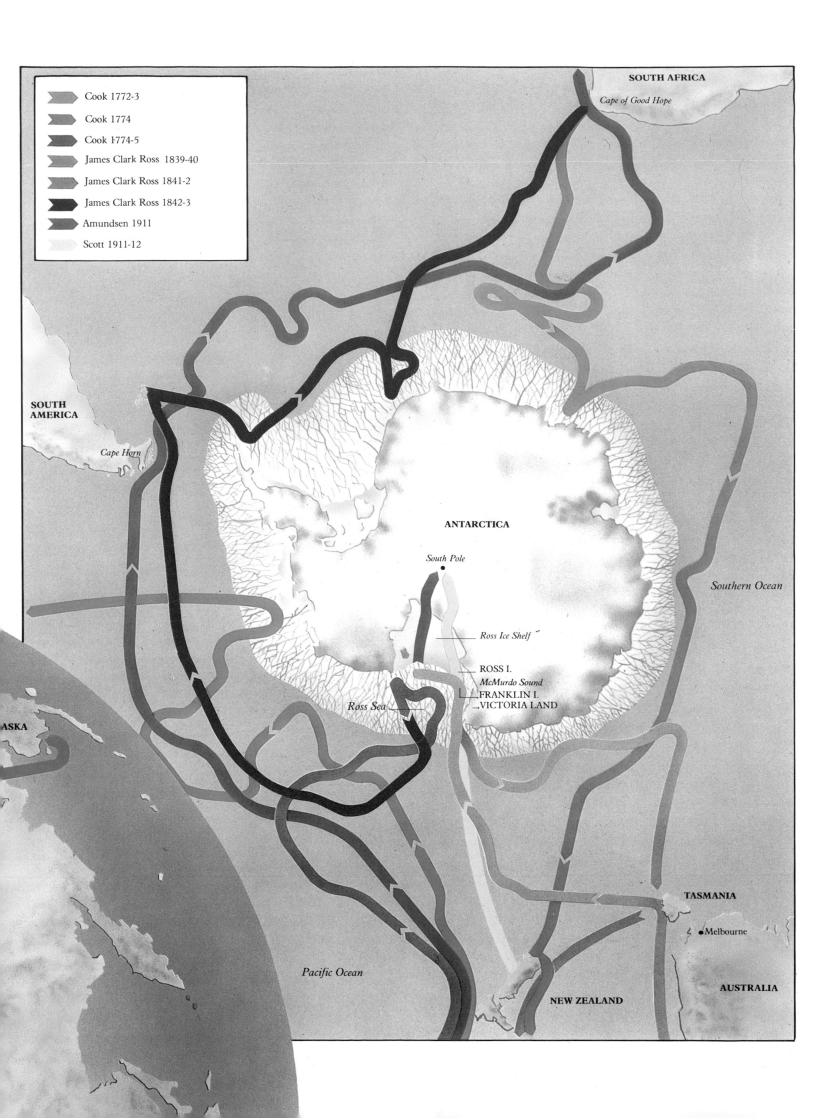

Cook 1772-3	
Cook 1774	
Cook 1774-5	
James Clark Ross 1839-40	
James Clark Ross 1841-2	
James Clark Ross 1842-3	
Amundsen 1911	
Scott 1911-12	

SOUTH AFRICA

Cape of Good Hope

SOUTH AMERICA

Cape Horn

ANTARCTICA

South Pole

Southern Ocean

Ross Ice Shelf

ROSS I.

McMurdo Sound

FRANKLIN I.

VICTORIA LAND

Ross Sea

ASKA

TASMANIA

Melbourne

Pacific Ocean

AUSTRALIA

NEW ZEALAND

John Franklin

(1786 – 1847)

The largest oilfield in North America is up in the Arctic Circle at Prudhoe Bay. In 1976, at Prudhoe's Dead Horse Airport, a plaque was erected to commemorate Sir John Franklin:

Franklin Memorial Plaque
Prudhoe Bay
150 years from that day
August 16, 1826
When Sir John Franklin discovered Prudhoe Bay
and encamped at Return Reef
Roderic Owen, a Franklin descendant
unveiled this memorial in the presence of
the Honourable Lowell Thomas JR.,
Lieutenant Gov.
of Alaska, and the Honourable Eben Hopson,
mayor
of the North Slope Borough
August 16, 1976.

The plaque could hardly be expected to mention that the journey from England to Prudhoe, which had taken John Franklin a year and a half, had taken his great-great-great-nephew flying over the North Pole, no more than one day.

The timely honour paid by British Petroleum to that great Arctic explorer, John Franklin, did not pass without some questioning. Who was Franklin? Why wasn't he better known; or rather, as well known as he had obviously once been? A map of North America shows the vast District of Franklin straddling the coastline of Canada and upwards amongst the frozen islands of the Arctic. Closer study reveals that in his two land expeditions Franklin and his parties mapped most of the northern rim of the American continent between Captain Cook's Icy Cape and the areas known to the Hudson's Bay Company round Wager River. Before Franklin, there were only two points charted – the mouth of the Coppermine and the mouth of the Mackenzie.

That Franklin as a naval man should lead two land expeditions seems odd. But so watery are the barren lands of the Arctic Circle that even today goods travel better by canoe than by the almost non-existent roads. In those days, he was considered the best man for the job. He was thirty-three and had already spent nearly twenty years in the navy, having fought at Trafalgar in the *Bellerophon*. He had sailed with his cousin, Matthew Flinders, to circumnavi-

gate Australia and had been on the 1818 Arctic voyage of Captain Buchan, which tried to reach the North Pole.

On his first land expedition in 1819 his party included a Doctor Richardson, a tough Scots seaman called John Hepburn, a draughtsman, George Back, and an assortment of French-Canadian *voyageurs*, iron-hard canoer-trappers. He had promises of assistance from the old-established Hudson's Bay Company (the HBC – 'Here Before Christ') and its rapidly growing rival, the North West Company. The idea was that, from the Great Slave Lake, he should go down the Coppermine River by canoe to the sea, and there, turning eastward, move on round the uncharted coast until he reached an HBC outpost towards Wager River. His journey was made in conjunction with a sea-borne expedition led by Lieutenant Edward Parry through Lancaster Sound, which was to work its way westward and southward until it met Franklin's land party or achieved a voyage through the North-west Passage. In fact Parry reached Melville Island, but was there stopped by mountainous walls of ice.

Opposite The Arctic at the mouth of the Coppermine River was drawn by George Black from first-hand experience.

Top This portrait of Franklin by W. Derby shows him in his prime as a naval officer.

Above Lieutenant Back's 'Manner of making a resting-place on a winter night' during Franklin's first expedition.

Top In 1851 engravings of a painting by Stephen Pearce of 'The Arctic council discussing the plan of search for Sir John Franklin for submission to the Lords of the Admiralty' went on sale to the public at two guineas a time.

fearful journey to his base camp. For the first few days they were able to shoot game, but when that became scarce they lived on scraps of rotten meat, bones and a lichen called *tripe-de-roche*, which is bitter to taste and induces diarrhoea. Men died, and one, the half-Iroquois Michel, turned cannibal and was shot by Dr Richardson. When at last they reached Fort Enterprise there was no sign of the promised stores; a small party set off to an Indian camp to get food and when they returned with supplies only four men remained alive. Back in England, Franklin became known as 'the man who ate his boots', but out there, to the Red Indian chief, Akaitcho, he was the man who, rather than kill a fly, would blow the half-gorged pest from his hands with a wry: 'The world is wide enough for us both.'

His second land expedition, again with Back and Richardson, set out from the Great Bear Lake down the Mackenzie and up the north slope of Alaska. Franklin got within about 150 miles of Point Barrow where he was to meet a ship-borne expedition. But winter showed signs of closing in, and in August 1826 at Return Reef, within sight of Prudhoe Bay, he decided to turn back. Richardson, heading another party which had left Franklin's and headed east, reached the mouth of the Coppermine River via the Arctic coast, thus linking the discoveries of Franklin's two voyages.

Thereafter the newly knighted Sir John Franklin, with his energetic second wife Jane, was forced to cool his heels: at first as a naval officer in the Mediterranean, then as governor of Van Diemen's Land, where a disagreement with the intrigues of local politicians and lack of support back in

Starting from his camp at Fort Enterprise in late spring 1821, Franklin reached the mouth of the Coppermine and duly turned right. But the coast did not stretch in an unbroken line eastward as Franklin had supposed and, by the time the 460 miles of Bathurst's Inlet had been reconnoitered, the party was dangerously short of supplies.

At Point Turnagain, on the eastern side of Bathurst's Inlet, he turned back for a

England led to a series of ludicrous scenes. Recalled with a degree of ignominy, he had the consolation of knowing that he was in line for the most determined assault yet on the North-west Passage.

Following the defeat of Napolcon in 1815, the men and ships of the Royal Navy, freed from active military service, were available to further the British Government's renewed interest in a search that had continued on and off since the fifteenth century. In earlier centuries men had conceived the idea of a short trade route to the commercial centres of the east, through the seas north and west of the newly discovered North American continent. By the middle of the nineteenth century the elusive North-west Passage had still not been found, and in 1845 Franklin, then aged fifty-eight, was chosen by the Admiralty to lead another expedition into the Arctic waters. In May that year, the ships *Erebus* and *Terror* were towed down the Thames to start the voyage to Greenland with every available aid then thought desirable, including barrels of lemon juice to combat scurvy.

Towards the end of July they were sighted by a whaling captain, made fast to an iceberg in Baffin Bay, where they had set up an observatory. On board were 129 officers and men, a female ape dressed by the crew in trousers and pet dogs called Old Neptune and Jacko – the usual sort of menagerie for those days. The captain dined with the ship's company, and reported that they had plenty of stores and were in excellent spirits. That was to be the last time they were seen alive.

Year after year, the Arctic was scoured by expedition after expedition sent to out to look for them: James Clark Ross with young Leopold McClintock (officially) in 1848; his uncle John Ross (unofficially); a government-sponsored voyage under the whaling master Penny; an American expedition by Grinnell; a further official expedition under Captain Austin; the one known as 'the last of the Arctic voyages' (official) by Belcher; and interspersed with these, Lady Franklin's several ventures financed with her own money and by public subscription. Over the decade following their disappearance, small trace was found of the crew and only gradually could an idea of their last movements be pieced together. They had visited Beechey Island and set up shooting-stations, ablutions and so on. They had even planted a garden – and then they had vanished.

Clairvoyants came forward. One was said

to materialise the spirit of a tiny child, 'Weasey' (Louisa) Coppin. When asked, 'Where is Sir John Franklin and how can he be reached?' tiny Weasey, through the medium of her ten-year-old sister Anne, who knew nothing of Arctic charts, was said to have seen to it that 'there immediately appeared on the opposite wall in large round-hand letters about 3 inches in height, the following: *Erebus and Terror, Lancaster Sound, Prince Regents Inlet, Point Victory, Victoria Channel.* Other

Above An engraving from a sketch by Lieutenant Hood, showing the interior of a Cree Indian tent. Hood was murdered by a French-Canadian Iroquois who intended eating him. Hood and the expedition's other artist, Back, nearly came to blows at Fort Enterprise over the favours of 'Green Stockings', one of their Red Indian guides.

Top HMS *Enterprise* entering Dolphin and Union Strait.

Above **They Forged the Last Link with their Lives**, an oil·painting by W. T. Smith (1895). Lieutenant Hobson, on McClintock's expedition in the *Fox* in search of Franklin, found a boat buried in the snow on the west coast of King William Island. Skeletons suggested that some sort of last stand had been made there – but against what, or whom, no one could tell.

alarms were frequent. Two derelict ships were seen clinging to an iceberg by a passenger on the brig *Renovation*. Might they have been *Erebus* and *Terror*, drifting on and on in grim fulfilment through the North-west Passage?

Even today, full details remain unknown. After the whaling captain left, the *Erebus* and *Terror* may have gone through Peel Sound and Franklin Strait, and then turned south-west into Victoria Strait. Franklin's mistaken charts here proved fatal, for they suggested that King William Island was joined at Poctes Bay to the Boothia Peninsula. He thus missed his chance of taking the passage east and south of the island (sometimes navigable because it is protected from the polar ice-stream flowing down from the Beaufort Sea) which Amundsen was later to find rewarding. Instead he put his ships into the dreaded

ice-stream on the unsheltered side of the island. Franklin was then less than 250 miles from Point Turnagain, south of Victoria Island, the furthest point of his own first land expedition.

What happened next we know from a message discovered by the last expedition sent by Lady Franklin in 1858, with Leopold McClintock commanding the *Fox*. It was found in a cairn at Point Victory on the north-west tip of King William Island:

April 25th, 1848 – HM ships *Terror* and *Erebus* were deserted on 22nd April, five leagues NNW of this, having been beset since 12th September 1846. The officers and crew, consisting of 105 souls, under the command of Captain F. R. M. Crozier landed here.... Sir John Franklin died on 11th June 1847; and the total loss by deaths in the expedition has been to this date 9 officers and 15 men.

Above *Doubling Cape Barrow* by Back. The thirty-five-mile gap between Cape Barrow and Cape Flinders involved the expedition in 450 miles of exploring Bathurst Inlet and Melville Sound, wasting so much of the short Arctic summer that they had to turn back prematurely.

those who forged the last link in the chain of the North-west Passage with their lives could only be guessed at. They had apparently met Eskimos (who had tales of cannibalism to tell the explorer Rae, though without adequate evidence). At best they had not been helped by Eskimos; at worst they'd been set upon and robbed. Scurvy did the rest, for by then the vitamin C of their lemon juice was fast losing its efficacy. Those who survived would have been mere rotting, walking skeletons.

Lady Franklin died just before the Franklin Memorial was unveiled in Westminster Abbey. Alfred, Lord Tennyson (who had married Franklin's niece), wrote the valediction:

Not here: the white North has thy bones; and thou,
Heroic sailor-soul,
Art passing on thine happier voyage now,
Towards no earthly pole.

Beneath that was the legend:

To the memory of Sir John Franklin, born April 16th, 1786, at Spilsby, Lincolnshire: died June 11th, 1847, off Point Victory, in the Frozen Ocean, the beloved chief of the crews who perished with him in completing the discovery of the North-West Passage. . . . This monument is erected by Jane, his widow, who, after long waiting and sending many in search of him, herself departed to find him in the realms of Life, July 18th, 1875, aged 83 years.

Later, a slab was added, announcing:

Here also is commemorated Admiral Sir Leopold M'Clintock, 1819–1907, discoverer of the fate of Franklin in 1859.

It was signed 'James Fitzjames, Captain HMS *Erebus*' and 'F. R. M. Crozier, Captain and Senior Officer'. A scrawled postscript announced: 'And start tomorrow, 26th, for Back's Fish River.' Stuck in the ice for over eighteen months, suffering from scurvy and with their rations running out, the crews had been carried slowly south, until Crozier gave orders to abandon ship.

The 105 survivors of the original 129 men set off across the ice, in the last stages of starvation and scurvy, supposedly hoping to reach the Hudson's Bay Company's post at Fort Resolution. But though some men reached bays further down the unsheltered west coast of King William Island (their bones and a boat were found) and others even crossed the narrow stretch of sea to the Canadian mainland, there to die in Starvation Cove, no records of the expedition were ever recovered. The fate of

John Ross (1777–1856) and James Clark Ross (1800–62)

It was a curious coincidence that both John Ross and his nephew James should each, when together on different Arctic explorations, have missed the chance of making an important discovery by mistaking a sea channel for a closed bay. After his first Arctic voyage in the *Isabella* in 1818, John Ross claimed that the imaginary 'Croker Mountains' lay right across the neck of Lancaster Sound. Parry (accompanied by Ross's nephew James) subsequently sailed right through the Sound and proved it to be an open channel. James, in his turn, took King William Island to be part of the mainland and named what was later proved to be a sheltered sea-channel down the eastern side, 'Poctes Bay'. Between 1903 and 1906 Amundsen sailed down that same sheltered east-coast channel to complete the first successful navigation of the North-west Passage.

John Ross's voyage in the *Isabella* had been part of a two-pronged Arctic expedition mounted by the Admiralty. Whilst he (with his young nephew) attempted the North-west Passage, Captain Buchan (with young John Franklin) was to aim for the North Pole. Since both attempts were accounted failures, another sea expedition led by Edward Parry was sent out the following year in conjunction with a land

Above 'Some cottages of the Boothians,' from John Ross's own book.

Top John Ross, the uncle.

Opposite Hope Bay, Antarctica.

153

expedition led by Franklin. Having sailed right through Lancaster Sound and reached Melville Island on his first voyage, Parry was commissioned to undertake two more voyages which provided valuable information about the Arctic seas but failed to find the North-west Passage. James Ross sailed with Parry on all three of these voyages as well as Parry's unsuccessful attempt on the Pole – when they made the shattering discovery that the ice-floes they were traversing with sledge-boats were drifting south faster than they were making progress north.

In 1828 John Ross submitted a new plan to the Admiralty, to search for the North-west Passage in Prince Regent Inlet. The Admiralty were unimpressed, having not yet forgotten the 'Croker Mountains', and Ross had to find a sponsor in the gin distiller, Felix Booth. In May, accompanied by his nephew James, Ross set out in the *Victory*, a paddle steamer rigged for sail.

Uncle and nephew made a far from harmonious team, cooped up together for three years in the same cabin with one 'attempting a few chords on the fiddle' and the other glowering and shivering in the opposite corner. But James, an experienced sailor and expert on magnetism who had already spent several winters in the Arctic, was nevertheless an invaluable member of the expedition.

There were considerable achievements to show for the voyage. In August they reached Prince Regent Inlet and, sailing south, landed on a peninsula which they named 'Boothia', after their patron. After wintering at Felix Harbour, where the Eskimos drew them maps of doubtful value and taught them how to make sledges, James struck out across land and ice to reach Point Victory, at the north-west tip of King William Island. He did not have enough stores with him to attempt the 250 miles which would have brought him to Franklin's Point Turnagain, and which would have solved the problem of the North-west Passage once and for all. Returning across the ice between King William Island and Boothia, he thought he saw land to the south and marked it as such on his chart, a mistake that would cost Franklin dear.

Throughout 1830 the *Victory* remained beset in the ice and in the spring of 1831 James Ross made another overland expedition. At 70° 5′N, 96° 46′W he found that magnetic needles did not move when suspended. He had made his great discovery of the expedition: the North Magnetic Pole.

154

In 1832, after three years trapped in the ice, John Ross was forced to abandon his ship and take his party on a terrible journey on foot and in small boats northwards up Prince Regent Inlet. Supplies from a ship abandoned by Parry on his third voyage saved them from starvation, but they were forced to spend another winter in the ice before they were eventually picked up in Lancaster Sound by a whaler, which turned out to be John Ross's old ship, the *Isabella*.

John Ross was knighted in 1834 and later became a rear-admiral, his reputation vindicated. He had managed to return from four winters in the Arctic with all but three of his men, and with a great deal of new information about the geography and meteorology of the Arctic.

James Ross went from strength to strength. When the British Government organized a naval expedition to go south to the Antarctic to study terrestrial magnetism, the discoverer of the North Magnetic Pole, who had so much experience of Arctic conditions, was the

obvious commander to choose. His instructions were to set up magnetic observatories on St Helena, the Cape of Good Hope, Kerguelen Island and Tasmania, and then to 'proceed directly to the southward in order to determine the position of the magnetic pole. . . .'

Ross and Captain Crozier set sail in 1839, in *Erebus* and *Terror*, two specially reinforced ships of 370 tons and 340 tons respectively. (*Terror* had already been in the Arctic and both were to go to the Arctic again on Franklin's last expedition.) Arriving in Van Diemen's Land (Tasmania) he found Franklin installed as governor, and 200 convicts were set to work on the new observatory, from which magnetic observations were soon being made, according to Franklin's niece Sophy Cracroft, 'once every month during twenty-four hours and . . . every quarter for the same time every two and a half minutes – the latter, simultaneously with every observatory in the world.'

In the summer of 1841–2 Ross and Crozier sailed into the Antarctic, and became the first men ever to venture into its pack-ice. After four days the waters cleared, and they found themselves in a great unknown sea, now called the Ross Sea. Two days later a dark, thousand-foot cliff loomed over them, the north-eastern point of what Ross called Victoria Land, and on 27 January, eighty miles from there, they landed on 'Franklin Island', spotting

Above Ross the nephew killing a musk bull at Umingmak. Abandoning the paddle-steamer *Victory* to the Arctic ice, uncle and nephew took to boats and were lucky enough to encounter a whaler off Navy Board Inlet: the whaler turned out to be the *Isabella*, which John Ross had captained on a previous voyage.

the 12,400 foot smoking volcano (Mount Erebus) on 'Ross Island' in the distance.

Ross was now only 160 miles from the South Magnetic Pole, but turning south to find it, his way was blocked by the great Ross Ice Shelf: solid ice covering an area larger than France and varying in thickness from 600 to 2000 feet. Assaults on the South Pole would later be mounted from this point, but Ross decided to turn back to Tasmania.

On his return to Van Diemen's Land, a formal ball was held on board the ships, at which Franklin was guest of honour. Back again in the Antarctic, beset in pack-ice, the New Year's Day found them holding a traditional sailors' ball. Festivities grew hectic: according to the ship's surgeon:

The two captains made their appearance under a rather irregular salute of musketry from a party of men rigged as a guard of honour, and took their seats upon a raised snow sofa, and soon after the ball commenced. Of course Capt. Crozier and Miss Ross opened the ball with a quadrille . . . you would have laughed to see the whole of us with thick overall boots on, dancing, waltzing and slipping about. . . .

Soon after, the rudders of both ships were smashed when *Erebus* rammed *Terror* in a commotion in the ice at night. After repairs in the Falkland Islands a third attempt at skirting the ice-pack met with moderate success until, after drifting in the pack, they made their way back to England

in 1843. James was knighted the following year.

James Ross would have been the obvious choice for Franklin's expedition to discover the North-west Passage in 1845, but he had apparently promised his new wife he would not go. He was the choice of the British Government in 1848 for the first official relief expedition, although his uncle claimed that Franklin had asked *him* to go in search of him. In *Enterprise* and *Endeavour*, with McClintock as lieutenant, James Ross wintered at the top of Prince Regent Inlet and sent parties down it. But he never tried to reach his own furthest point, Point Victory on King William Island: had he done so, he would have been too late to save the men, but valuable records might have been preserved.

John Ross eventually mounted his own fruitless search for Franklin, again with financial backing from Booth. At well over seventy, it was remarkable that he should be in the Arctic at all. Felix Booth died and on his return Ross found himself badly in debt. The worry of it was much on his mind until his own death in 1856.

His nephew James lived long enough to hear of the success of his former lieutenant, McClintock, in discovering the Franklin message in the cairn at Point Victory. But from it he also learned the terrible fate of his friend Captain Crozier, who had taken command after Franklin's death.

Below The occasion described as 'First Communication with the Natives of Prince Regents Bay, as drawn by John Sackheouse and presented to Capt. Ross, August 10, 1818'. Prince Regent Inlet was thought to provide a possible route through the long-sought-after North-west Passage. And so it did, via the Bellot Strait; but there turned out to be other, better ways through the Arctic.

Fridtjof Nansen
(1861 – 1930)

Above Fridtjof Nansen, from his book *Farthest North*. Nansen chose to go about the streets of Stockholm in winter without an overcoat, wearing a tight fitting dark blue jersey-like blouse or jacket which 'made some people think he was an acrobat'.

Previous page Sea ice in the Arctic.

'If you can't beat them, join them!' is not the sort of saying which springs to mind when considering the methods of great explorers. Nevertheless, humble adaptability has often served those adventuring into the unknown better than inflexible determination. It was an article of faith with Vilhjalmur Stefansson, the explorer and ethnologist, that the Arctic, one of the most inhospitable areas known to man, was 'friendly', if a man would only try and work with, not against it; his successes proved his point. Parry in his polar voyage had been dismayed to find that a drift to the south pushed his boat-sledge back faster than it could move north. Nansen in 1893 decided to use this drawback the better to achieve his purpose; which was, to drift, deliberately beset in the high Arctic icestream, right across the North Pole. When this didn't work (they were drifting all right, but it wasn't across the Pole), he left his frozen-in *Fram* and set off with one companion and a dog-sledge. When that didn't work, he retreated, survived the winter in an igloo on seal and bear meat and was lucky enough to be picked up, by

chance, by an expedition not specifically trying to look for him.

He was by then already a national hero. As a very young man, dispassionately viewing his own nature, he had decided to follow the side he called 'Mr Irresponsible', leaving 'the quiet life of science' to go on an Arctic sealing voyage. Science was in the ascendant for his next six years of zoology, but (as with Sven Hedin) Adolf Nordenskiöld's triumphant completion of the North-east Passage set him afire for an exploit of his own – crossing Greenland, on skis, from east to west. It was an all-Norwegian venture, at a time when emergent Norwegian nationalism required exactly that. The enforced union of Sweden and Norway under Bernadotte had led to a ferment of unrest and frenzied desire for a sop to national pride.

Starting from an uninhabited 'nowhere', Nansen's crossing of Greenland ended up amongst the Eskimos at Cape Bille. Throughout their journey, he and his companions had no line of retreat. It was go forward or die, coming to terms with each problem as it arose.

Left Fram in the ice. Nansen's ship was specially designed to ride up over the ice as soon as she began being nipped and squeezed. Thereafter he intended making use of 'Arctic drift' to bring him to the North Pole. He very nearly succeeded.

Below When drifting in *Fram*, in pack-ice, Nansen was careful to carry out scientific research on some scale. Here he is shown flanked by members of his crew observing the eclipse of the sun on 6 April 1894.

For his famous 'drifting' voyage of 1893 the boat he had specially built to ride up with the ice was hopefully called the *Fram* – 'forward'. A visit to England the year before to drum up interest and money had met with admiration but disbelief. Sir Leopold McClintock, the president, said that it was 'the most daring plan ever laid before the Royal Geographical Society'; but he did not personally think that any ship could be made strong enough to resist the irresistible pressures of the pack-ice. Others were even more pessimistic. The American, General Greely, castigated it as 'an illogical scheme of self-destruction'.

However, with Otto Sverdrup (who had been with him on the Greenland expedition) and eleven others, Nansen put his scheme to the test. The *Fram* set out for the Kara Sea and points north of the New Siberian Islands. Their stores were excellent. Clothing was revolutionary – woollen underwear and light wind-proof outer garments instead of skins and furs. They also took dogs and dog-sledges, kayaks and the Norwegian flag.

In September Nansen achieved his first

object: the *Fram* was beset in the ice. In October the ice started to pack. On 13 October he wrote:

Now we are in the very midst of what the prophets would have us dread so much. The ice is pressing and packing round us with a noise like thunder ... in fact it is trying its very utmost to grind the *Fram* into powder. But here we sit quite tranquil, not even going up to look at all the hurly-burly, but just chatting and laughing as usual.

With electricity supplied by a wind-driven dynamo, the *Fram* became a busy, floating scientific laboratory. They studied all of the elements around them: the currents, temperature and salinity of the water; the formation and thickness of the ice; and the electricity in the air. Every four hours they took meteorological observations, and every second day they took astronomical observations to determine their position and the direction of their drift. They collected underwater specimens, and tested their own blood every month. All the same, by the first week in November, *Fram* was back where she started. And it was just as disappointing again, next year, when they reached no more than 83° North. Nansen could not bear to 'sit quite tranquil' any longer.

In the spring of 1895 he planned a breakout over the ice to the North Pole for himself and one companion, Frederik Johansen, with twenty-eight dogs and plenty of provisions of powdered and dried fish and meat, biscuits and butter. After a great deal of soul-searching, Nansen decided to leave the others behind in the *Fram* to go drifting on, beset in ice; a decision for which he was later much criticized. In fact, Sverdrup and the rest said that they were quite happy to be left as they were, about 350 miles south of the North Pole.

The dreadful ice formations, the lumps and bumps and saw-toothed edges, blocked Nansen and Johansen's progress. Nansen wrote:

Our hearts fail us when we see the ice lying before us like an impenetrable maze of ridges, lanes, brash and huge blocks thrown together pell-mell.... There are moments when it seems impossible that any creatures not possessed of wings can get further and one longingly follows the flight of a passing gull.

The coming of a spring thaw beat them. On the evening of 24 March they killed their first dog, the idea being to save stores by feeding the surviving dogs on those they butchered. Nansen's daughter wrote: 'The killing of them was the most unpleasant

experience of the whole trip; and for a long time the dogs refused to eat their own dead. They had to be really famished before they could be induced to accept their own kind.' In April, melting ice forced them to turn back when at 86° 13'N. At the beginning of August they reached open sea and then, with heavy hearts, they shot the remaining two dogs – 'faithful and enduring, they had toiled with us all that long while, and now, when better times were in prospect, they had to say goodbye to life'. There was no room for dogs in the boat, made of two kayaks lashed together, in which they put to sea and reached Franz Josef Land.

It was eleven months later – months of adapting to circumstances, of hibernation in an igloo heated with walrus blubber and a further journey in their makeshift craft –

that they reached safety. On one occasion the kayaks broke loose from their moorings and drifted swiftly away with all they possessed on board. Nansen dived into the icy water in pursuit, but soon felt his limbs growing numb. He afterwards admitted that these were the worst moments he had ever lived through, knowing that whether he sank or turned back without the kayaks, the result would be the same. Fortunately, he managed to reach them but was so stiff and cold he could hardly paddle them back.

A few days later they heard the bark of a dog and saw a dark figure moving amongst the hummocks. Nansen wrote: 'I recognized Mr Jackson, whom I remembered once to have seen. I raised my hat: we extended a hand to one another with a hearty "How do you do?" It was some time before Jackson said: "Aren't you Nansen?" and was told: "Yes I am".'

Jackson was an Englishman on the Jackson-Harmsworth expedition of 1894. He carried letters for Nansen, in case of just such an eventuality. In Jackson's relief ship, the *Windward*, Nansen and Johansen reached Vardö in comfort. On that very day, 13 August, the *Fram* drifted free of the ice near Spitzbergen.

From then on, Nansen was Norway's great hero; perhaps too much so for his own contentment. Instead of pressing on with his ideas of going to the North or South Pole, he allowed himself to be side-tracked into oceanographic research and politics. In 1905 the vexed question of Norwegian nationalism bubbled up again; it led to a plebiscite and an invitation to Prince

Above Strange light-effects, such as this 'moon-ring' sketched by Nansen, were commonplace in the Arctic sky, but never ceased to inspire Nansen and his companions with awe.

Charles of Denmark to accept the Norwegian throne as 'Haakon VII'. Nansen was sent to England as the first Norwegian minister; a thoroughly popular appointment, but for him, not right. 'These court functions are incredible,' he wrote. 'They are so pointless they become almost interesting.' But all this was at the expense of another exploring adventure.

Things came to a head when Amundsen persuaded him to let him borrow the *Fram* for an expedition to the North Pole in 1910: it was as good as declaring that he himself was finished. When Amundsen made a dash instead for the South Pole, without informing his backers, the Fram Committee, Nansen could hardly rejoice. Yet he congratulated Amundsen on his return 'on a job well done' and defended him against detractors. 'What it cost me to give up what I had so long planned and immersed myself in, not even I realized till afterwards,' he wrote to Amundsen in 1913. 'Though I never let you notice it, I hope.'

Nansen worked hard for the League of Nations and for First World War refugees; his compassion and humanitarian devotion to duty earned him the Nobel Peace Prize in 1922.

When elected Lord Rector of the University of St Andrew's in 1926 – the first foreigner for that honour – he said in his address to the undergraduates: '"Becoming famous and enriched" is not life's purpose or goal. It is not as easy as that. You have come into the world to do your share and to do it well wherever you find yourselves.' Impeccable sentiments for the occasion; but perhaps he meant it more when he muttered to his daughter, in his old age: 'Better a great sinner provided he has a heart, than these people who pride themselves on being so immaculate!'. He had always been, in his own way, a man of soul-searching and humility; yet all ambition had not been quenched. He still wanted to get to the North Pole, even if it meant flying there in a Zeppelin; he even became chairman of an Arctic Society to promote the idea. In 1928 he signed a contract with the German government and lectured in the States to raise funds. His expedition might have got off the ground in the spring of 1930, but he grew feeble and died on 13 May.

Above The meeting of Jackson and Nansen. Nansen and Johansen had almost given up hope of seeing another human being again when they met Jackson of the Jackson-Harmsworth expedition.

Top Walruses provided food, and Nansen and Johansen used the blubber to heat their igloo. Nansen's sketch shows the end of a successful hunt, but the quarry could be savage and had intelligence enough to overturn the boats of their attackers by coming up under them.

Robert Peary (1856–1920) and Frederick Cook (1865–1940)

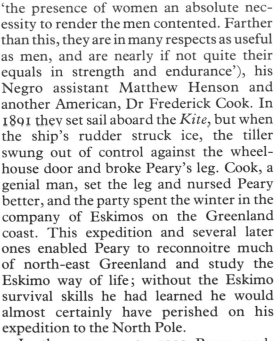

Above Itching for fame, Robert Peary happened to come across Nordenskiöld's *Exploration of Inner Greenland* in a second-hand bookshop in Washington, and from that time was determined to be the first man to reach the North Pole.

Previous page Crossing a lead in the ice in boats.

Robert Peary was extraordinarily courageous, determined and competitive. To Nansen exploration was for the purpose of scientific enquiry; to Peary it was a race. His ambition was to rival the fame of Christopher Columbus, which could be equalled 'only by him who shall one day stand with 360° of longitude beneath his motionless foot, for whom East and West shall have vanished: the discoverer of the North Pole'.

He first ventured into the Arctic in 1886 when, as a young US naval officer, he attempted to make the 500-mile journey across Greenland and was forced by bad weather to turn back after 125 miles.

Peary's party for a second attack on Greenland included his wife Jo (in 1885 Peary wrote that on expeditions he found 'the presence of women an absolute necessity to render the men contented. Farther than this, they are in many respects as useful as men, and are nearly if not quite their equals in strength and endurance'), his Negro assistant Matthew Henson and another American, Dr Frederick Cook. In 1891 they set sail aboard the *Kite*, but when the ship's rudder struck ice, the tiller swung out of control against the wheelhouse door and broke Peary's leg. Cook, a genial man, set the leg and nursed Peary better, and the party spent the winter in the company of Eskimos on the Greenland coast. This expedition and several later ones enabled Peary to reconnoitre much of north-east Greenland and study the Eskimo way of life; without the Eskimo survival skills he had learned he would almost certainly have perished on his expedition to the North Pole.

In the years up to 1900 Peary made several unsuccessful attempts on the Pole, during one of which the temperature fell to −50° Centigrade (−58° Fahrenheit) and eight of his toes had to be amputated because of severe frostbite.

With each attempt he became more determined, enlisting the aid of the Peary Arctic Society, of congressmen and of the

president, and having a ship, the *Theodore Roosevelt*, built to his specifications. The hull was two feet thick and reinforced with steel, and the rudder was retractable, so that the vessel would be able to force a passage through the Robeson Channel to the north-east coast of Ellesmere Island.

In 1905 the attempt was made, the *Theodore Roosevelt* forced a passage to Ellesmere Island and was within 186 miles of the Pole when the temperature fell so sharply that the expedition had to turn back, with only the satisfaction of knowing that no one had ever before been so close to the Pole. The next three years were spent in preparation for a final try.

Meanwhile Frederick Cook had been to the Arctic as surgeon on a Belgian expedition (which included Roald Amundsen as first mate). After that he led an expedition which he claimed as the first successful assault on Mount McKinley in Alaska. Then, supported by the Explorers' Club – rivals to the Peary Arctic Club – he conceived his own plan for reaching the North Pole.

His assault on the North Pole, in March–April 1908, organized on similar lines to Peary's, using Eskimo dress, food and skills, was a once-only effort on a very small scale. Using the yacht owned by and named after his patron John R. Bradley, he sailed to a place in Greenland, north of Etah, called Annoatok. Leaving stores behind in the care of Rudolph Francke he set out with four Eskimos. After some three-score miles, two of the Eskimos were sent back and Cook and two Eskimos only went on, with sledges and twenty-six dogs, for the 460 miles which lay between them and the Pole. Twenty of the dogs were regarded as expendable, to be killed one by one to provide fresh meat.

Fearful adventures and mishaps followed: one time, Cook awoke to find himself in freezing water, the ice cracking under his igloo. All the same, by 30 March they had no more than 300 miles to go: by 19 April, twenty-nine miles. At midnight

Above Frederick Cook, American doctor son of a German immigrant doctor, went to the Antarctic as a surgeon in a ship which included Roald Amundsen as first mate. Amundsen found him 'very much a man' but later others called him a charlatan.

Above left Peary believed in leap-frogging his stores support, sending parties like this on ahead to establish depots for parties in the rear going in turn on ahead. He thus ensured that he himself travelled unencumbered and at speed. In the autumn, for hunting and transporting supplies, tents were used as shelter. For winter travelling and the sledge journey the party built igloos.

Robert Peary and Frederick Cook

on 21 April the three of them raised the Stars and Stripes over an igloo on the ice and buried a note in a metal tube: 'I felt like some watcher of the skies when a new planet swims into his ken,' Cook quoted from Keats. On the return journey, Cook had to winter beyond Devon Island, at Cape Sparbo; so he did not reach Annoatok until the following spring. There – he said – he left his papers behind before taking ship from Egedesminde to Copenhagen, sending his first messages about his dash to the Pole while on the voyage from Lerwick.

Peary's progress in 1908 was, meanwhile, on a very different scale. Aboard the *Roosevelt*, he and his well-equipped team steamed off to Cape York, where they took on board Eskimos and over 100 dogs. At Etah, he found evidence of Cook's visit the year before – stores, still being guarded by Francke. Peary wrote bitterly to his backers, complaining that Cook was 'out for the admitted purpose of stealing a march on me'. It was as if he regarded the whole Arctic as his personal property. He feared that Cook had snaffled dogs which might otherwise have been available for him; he was even afraid that Cook might have 'spoiled' the Eskimos by getting them used to American luxuries, which was why he set a special guard of his own on the doctor's stores. Early in March, he left from Cape Columbia, 420 miles from the Pole. As always he sent teams of Eskimos ahead to establish igloo camps and stores of food along the route. The provisions were mostly pemmican, both for dogs and men, tea, hard tack and condensed milk.

In temperatures as low as any he had known, crossing leads (channels) on rafts of ice, Peary and his companions battled northwards. At 86° 38′ North one of his companions turned back – tragically he fell into the ice and died. At 88°, on 1 April, another of the party left. Peary, with five sledges, Henson, four Eskimos and thirty-eight dogs, headed north for 140 miles. The wind was 'keen and bitter as frozen steel', and Peary was tortured by pain from the leg set by Frederick Cook in 1891, which had never troubled him until that moment. Leads in the ice opened and closed, whilst bright sunlight gave place to 'a dense lifeless pall of gray overhead, almost black at the horizon'.

On 6 April they camped and Peary brought out a small taffeta flag. Henson asked what the camp was to be called. 'The last and most northerly camp on earth,' said Peary, erecting the flag on top of their igloo.

After they had taken observations, Peary looked satisfied; in his diary he wrote: 'The pole at last!!! The prize of three centuries, my dream and ambition for twenty-three years. *Mine* at last.' They took soundings and found the sea was over 1500 fathoms deep. They were standing on a desolate, shifting sea of ice. The North Pole was not a fixed spot at all. It and their flag would drift away leaving not a trace behind. Even so, it was Peary's moment of triumph:

... In a march of only a few hours, I had passed from the western to the eastern hemisphere and had verified my position at the summit of the world. ... East, west and north had disappeared for us. Only one direction remained, and that was south. Every breeze which could possibly blow upon us, no matter from what point of the horizon, must be a south wind.

Above 'A typical example of the difficulties of working sledges over a pressure ridge', a photograph of the expedition from Peary's book *The North Pole* (1910).

Opposite above Peary's party 'at the Pole'. The party consisted of four Eskimos, thirty-eight dogs, five sledges – and Henson (standing centre), his Negro companion/ servant.

Opposite below Both Peary and Cook claimed to have reached the North Pole first. This picture hedges its bets by showing them together, as 'Discoverers of the North Pole'.

On the way back, the men killed and ate some of their faithful dogs, and in August were back on board *Roosevelt* at Cape Chalon. It was there that they learnt about Cook and his claims.

Peary declared to the *New York Times*: 'He [Cook] has not been to the Pole on 21 April 1908, or at any other time. He has simply handed the public a gold brick.' A former governor of Atlanta retorted, 'If Cook has handed us a gold brick, Peary has handed us a paste diamond.' The public appeared to agree. The *Pittsburg Press* conducted a poll; the results were: Cook discovered the North Pole in 1908, 73,238 votes; Peary discovered the North Pole in 1909, 2,814 votes; Cook did not reach Pole, 2,814 votes; Peary did not reach Pole, 58,009 votes. The editor commented, 'The curious thing about it is that 58,009 persons should believe that Peary did not reach the Pole merely because he had treated ungraciously a man who was trying to rob him of his glory'.

Backed by the weight of established authority, Peary eventually prevailed in the controversy that ensued. He had reached the Pole: there was no doubt about that. And if Frederick Cook had not insisted that he had been there first, Peary might have been able to admit that he too had reached the Pole. Neither emerged from the debate with much credit. As the explorer Peter Freuchen remarked, 'Cook was a liar and a gentleman. Peary was neither.'

In 1911 an article (which the editors had deliberately distorted, according to its stenographer) purported to give a confession by Cook: 'On mature reflection . . . I do not know absolutely whether I reached the Pole or not'. During the next years the admittedly eccentric doctor made appearances in vaudeville as a mimic and acrobat. He then kept out of the limelight until 1923, when he received a long jail sentence for alleged misrepresentation of facts about oil-leases in Texas. In 1940, however, as he lay dying, he rallied enough to hear that he had been granted a full pardon by President Roosevelt. By that time, Peary had long been dead; pernicious anaemia had carried him off in 1920. The controversy between the two men proved one thing: the importance to explorers of keeping proper records, if they want to avoid being called charlatans.

Roald Amundsen (1872–1928) and Robert Falcon Scott (1868–1912)

A flag waving from the South Pole possessed this advantage over one planted at the pole at the other end of the world – instead of drifting away on ice it stayed still on land. For Scott, this was unfortunate; what should have been his moment of greatest triumph turned, at the blink of a sore eyelid, into defeat. At the North Pole, the chances were, he might not have known that another had been there first.

Unlike so many great explorers, Scott's inclination towards Antarctic adventure was not something earnestly sought from childhood. As a young naval officer, expert in surveying, his career was steady and dependable and might have continued as such had he not happened to engage the interest of Sir Clements Markham, president of the Royal Geographical Society and veteran of the Franklin search, who had by now turned his attention to the Antarctic. Waiting to mount an expedition to make a detailed scientific survey of the continent, he asked George Egerton, captain of the *Majestic*, in which Scott was a lieutenant, what he thought of Scott for an expedition leader. 'Just the fellow for it, strong, steady, genial, scientific, a good head on his shoulders, and a very good naval officer.'

Others were clustering as thick as bees round the idea of reaching the extreme south of the world. Bull, in the *Antarctic*: Borchgrevink, in the *Southern Cross*: de Gerlache, in the *Belgica*: a German expedition under von Drygalski: a Swedish expedition under Nordenskiöld: even a Scottish one under Bruce. Markham was forced to indulge in devious in-fighting to promote his man Scott, indeed his entire scheme. The ever-present problem of funds was partly solved by a huge donation from Llewellyn Longstaff, a paint manufacturer, which included a request, with the force virtually of an order, to employ his son's friend, Ernest Shackleton.

The *Discovery*, the ship specially built for the National Antarctic Expedition, was soon probing about in Ross Sea alongside the Great Ice Barrier (now called the Ross Ice Shelf), trying to find shelter. McMurdo Sound seemed the best. Under the protecting promontory of Hut Point, winter quarters were established in February 1902. Summer sledging in the Antarctic could not start until September; and even that was rather too early.

No one could understand why scurvy struck three of them in October. Tainted meat was thought to be the cause, but all their tinned meat had been opened under

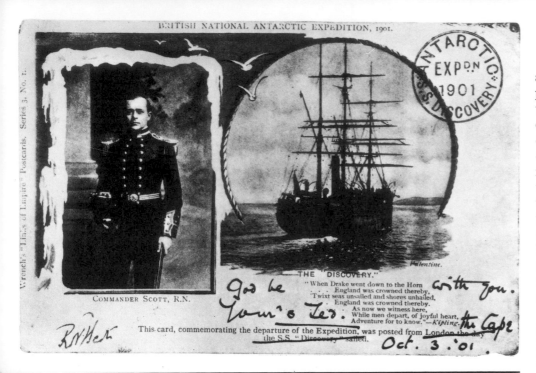

COMMANDER SCOTT, R.N.

THE "DISCOVERY."

"When Drake went down to the Horn
England was crowned thereby,
Twixt seas unsailed and shores unhailed,
England was crowned thereby.
As now we witness here,
While men depart, of joyful heart,
Adventure for to know."—*Kipling*.

This card, commemorating the departure of the Expedition, was posted from London the day the S.S. "Discovery" sailed.

God be with you.
Yours Ted.
R.N. Scott
the Cape
Oct. 3. '01.

Above As a cavalry officer, Captain Oates loved horses and knew how to handle them. Scott took Manchurian ponies as beasts of burden for his expedition, against the advice of Nansen, who much preferred to use dogs.

Top A commemorative card from the British National Antarctic Expedition.

Previous pages Icebergs in winter sea-ice off Signy Island, South Orkneys.

strictest supervision. As a precaution, seals were slaughtered to provide fresh meat (a thing Scott, who loved animals, disliked doing) and bottled fruit and lime-juice rations were increased. Shackleton succumbed and had to be sent back in the relief ship *Morning*. Then there was trouble with the dogs; they suffered on the diet of frozen fish, lost much of their natural zest and one by one they died; with them went the party's chance of reaching the Pole, though the scientific work went on apace.

At the top of the Ferrar Glacier, 8900 feet above sea level, beyond Desolation Camp, Scott wrote: 'Before us lay the unknown. What fascination lies in that word. Could

anyone wonder that we are determined to push on?' And of his men: 'What children these men are! And yet what splendid children! They won't give in till they break down and then they consider their lapse disgraceful.' But on beyond there was nothing but 'a further expanse of our terrible plateau'. By 31 December 1902 they had advanced 300 miles further south than any other mortal and realized they could go no further. Turning round, they began the dispiriting march back, with only enough food left to last a fortnight. It was twenty-eight days before they reached a supply depot.

In 1904 Scott and his men returned to England and a hearty welcome. Scott was honoured with the patron's medal of the Royal Geographical Society and an invitation to Balmoral from the king. He met influential people including the Frenchman, Jean Charcot, who, like him, hated the 'wanton destruction of wild life' which polar exploration so often entailed; Scott called him the 'gentleman of the Pole'. He met Sir James Barrie, author of *Peter Pan* and he met his future wife, Kathleen Bruce, the sculptress, whom he married in 1908, when he was forty. His book, *The Voyage of Discovery*, was dedicated to Markham – 'the father of the expedition and its most constant friend'.

There matters might have rested, as far as Scott was concerned. Shackleton, a younger man, waited for no one but struck back at the Antarctic with an expedition of his own, reaching within ninety-seven miles of the South Pole, casually making use of Scott's winter quarters in spite of giving assurances that he would not; and, much to Markham's fury, soaking up money from prospective Antarctic patrons.

Scott, however, took matters into his own hands, writing to Shackleton to inform him that he intended to go to the South Pole, and plunging into a campaign of fund-raising to buy the *Terra Nova*. He sought Nansen's opinion over his plan to use Manchurian ponies to haul the sledges, and ignored his advice to use dogs instead. 'Suppose you don't succeed at first?' he was asked. 'We shall jolly well stop there till the thing is done,' he replied.

On 1 June 1910 he set sail with the members of his team, including Lieutenant Edward Evans, his second-in-command, Lawrence ('Titus') Oates, an old Etonian cavalry officer, Dr Edward Wilson, one of Scott's closest friends, Lieutenant Bowers and Apsley Cherry-Garrard. Their equipment and clothing, apart from three motor sledges, were conventional Navy gear. Amundsen, who like Peary had studied the Eskimo way of life, was to prove to be much more practically and efficiently equipped.

The *Terra Nova* arrived in Melbourne, Australia, on 10 October 1910, in good time to cross the Antarctic Circle at about Christmas, the height of the Antarctic summer. There a telegram was handed to Scott: 'Beg leave inform you proceeding Antarctic. Amundsen.'

Unlike Scott, Roald Amundsen had been dedicated to exploration ever since the age of fifteen, when he had read about Franklin eating his boots.

Strangely enough, the thing in Sir John's narrative that appealed to me most strongly was the sufferings he and his men endured. A strange ambition burned within me to endure those same sufferings. ... I irretrievably decided to be an Arctic explorer.

In 1897 he managed to get himself included in the Belgian Antarctic expedition on *Belgica*, which was beset for thirteen months, by which time scurvy was affecting the whole ship's company. Amundsen took over command and instantly made the eating of fresh meat compulsory – with dramatic effect upon the entire crew.

On his return, Amundsen sought out Nansen. Obtaining his backing, he bought a fishing boat, *Gjoa*, and left in a downpour a few hours ahead of his creditors for an attempt on the North-west Passage. Instead of heading into the semi-permanent ice-stream of Victoria Channel, he went round the sheltered, eastern side of King William Island. Thus he was the first actually to go by ship all the way through the North-west Passage.

He next persuaded Nansen to let him have the famous *Fram* for a 'drifting' attempt on the North Pole. But, 'just as everything was about ready, the world was electrified by the news that Admiral Peary, in April 1909, had reached the North Pole. This was a blow indeed,' wrote Amundsen. 'If I was to maintain my prestige as an explorer, I must quickly achieve a sensational success of some sort. . . . I resolved upon a coup.' When the *Fram* reached Madeira, he finally told his crew that he planned to go to the *South* Pole. They left a sealed envelope to be opened some days after they had sailed. In it were instructions for the notorious cable to be sent off to Scott in Australia. A race had begun, and the advantage lay with the challenger.

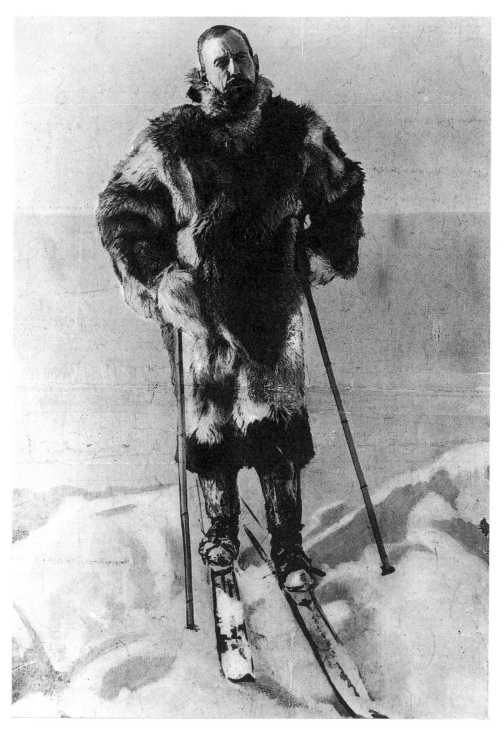

Scott could not start disembarking stores for the winter base in McMurdo Sound until January 1911. At Cape Evans he was fifteen miles from his old winter quarters at Hut Point, in which he found a solid block of ice had formed because Shackleton had carelessly left open a window. A week later Amundsen arrived in the Bay of Whales, sixty miles nearer to the Pole, and unloaded his dogs, sledges and stores. Like Peary, Amundsen used dog-teams to haul his sledges. He was also aware of the importance of fresh meat in his team's diet, and he came up with an efficient but callous plan to use his dogs both to pull the sledges and as a supply of fresh meat when necessary,

Above Roald Amundsen in working clothes. Amundsen's equipment was more practical than Scott's, owing to his careful study of Eskimo ways.

saying that he knew 'the precise day on which I planned to kill each dog as its usefulness should end for drawing the diminishing supplies on the sleds and its usefulness should begin as food for the men'. Amundsen's approach to the expedition was altogether more professional and ruthless than Scott's. His party consisted of eight men with 118 dogs, while Scott's party of thirty-three was supported by only thirty-three dogs and seventeen ponies.

By 17 February Scott had already lost five dogs and eight ponies, and, hampered by cumbersome equipment, was lagging behind Amundsen in making depots. The Norwegian party, making four and a half miles an hour on skis and with their light sledges hauled by dogs, forged ahead, leaving their final depot on 12 November. They were now in 84°S, and near the foot of the great Axel Heiberg Glacier, which they negotiated over the next two weeks. On 4 December they slaughtered forty dogs, and the weather began to worsen. A blizzard blew up against them, causing agonizing frost sores, and the temperature dropped to −43° Centigrade (−44° Fahrenheit). On 14 December they raised the Norwegian flag on the South Pole.

Meanwhile the Scott party was still battling on the Beardmore Glacier, just off the Ross Ice Shelf. As the ponies collapsed one by one and were reluctantly slaughtered, and the motor sledges broke down, Scott and his companions were compelled to trudge the 1532 miles to the Pole and back on foot, over the terrible glacier and up to 10,570 feet, before reaching the soft sandy snow and the rutted ice-crystals of the polar plateau.

Scott, Wilson, Oates, Evans and Bowers began their final assault on the Pole from Three Degree Depot, 178 miles from their goal, on 4 January. On 18 January they reached the Pole, to find a Norwegian flag fluttering from an abandoned sledge. The Norwegians had beaten them to it.

'Great God! This is an awful place, and terrible enough for us to have laboured to it without the reward of priority,' wrote Scott. They were tired and ill, and the wind blew keenly: 'Well, it is something to have got here, and the wind may be our friend tomorrow.' ('We have never had to move a foot; all we had to do was to let ourselves be towed along,' wrote Amundsen. 'The sledging was ideal and the weather beautiful.')

But the wind was not so well disposed towards Scott and his party. On the terrible

Opposite 'I'm just going outside and may be some time,' said Lawrence Oates as he left Scott and his companions in their tent, during a blizzard. They all knew he would not return. J. G. Dollman's picture is entitled: *A Very Gallant Gentleman*.

800-mile journey back to Cape Evans the five men dutifully continued to collect scientific specimens, despite their exhaustion. Oates and Evans were suffering from frostbite; Evans fell down a crevasse and afterwards seemed strangely affected until he died on 18 February. The cold was increasing, and by 6 March Oates was beginning to fail: his frostbitten feet had turned black, his toes bubbling with gangrene. On 10 March the north-west wind still blew and in the tent Scott gave out the rations of eternity, the thirty opium tablets with which each man could end his life. On they went, struggling towards the depot where there was food already stored, fifty miles and more away.

On 16 March Oates said he could not move. He asked to be left but the others refused and he managed one more day. Then, as they sat crouched in the tent, he said: 'I'm just going outside and may be some time.' And he went out into the blizzard. 'We knew that poor Oates was

walking to his death, but though we tried to dissuade him, we knew it was the act of a brave man and an English gentleman,' wrote Scott.

Two days later they made their last camp, hemmed in by the blizzard day after day. The end was very near for all of them. They had all, except Scott, given up making entries in their diaries, and on 29 March he wrote:

Every day we have been ready to start for our depot only eleven miles away, but outside of the tent it remains a scene of whirling drift. I do not think we can hope for any better things now. We shall stick it out to the end, but we are growing weaker, of course and the end cannot be far. . . . It seems a pity, but I do not think that I can write more. R. Scott. For God's sake look after our people.

He, the oldest, outlived them all. They were not found until November. Everything in the tent was tidy: the corpses of Wilson and Bowers looked strangely peaceful. The opium tablets had done their work.

But Scott lay half out of his sleeping-bag, one arm outflung towards Wilson. 'It was clear he had had a very hard last minutes,' said Tryggve Gran, one of those who eventually found the tent all but buried in the snow. Beside Scott were letters he had written to the wives of Wilson and Bowers, and to his own wife and son. His last concern was for the dependants of the members of his tragic expedition.

To a public guiltily aware of having done too little to support Scott, such a resounding, nobly-recorded defeat seemed almost preferable to the victory of Amundsen. Amundsen, denied the credit he felt was his due, was nonplussed: 'By and large, the British are a race of very bad losers,' he stated bitterly, 'What they call luck I prefer to call planning.' He visited England towards the end of 1912 and gave a lecture (Kathleen Scott found it 'modest but excessively dull'). Then, at the dinner given by the Royal Geographical Society, the president, Curzon, made a speech ending: 'I therefore propose three cheers for the dogs!' 'Clearly indicating the next moment the satirical and derogatory intention of the phrase by turning to me with an unnecessary calming gesture,' remarked Amundsen.

After the War, Amundsen saw the importance of the air – unfortunately a venture to fly to the North Pole ended in bankruptcy. However, in 1926, when he went for dirigibles, Lincoln Ellsworth, the American explorer, backed him. The flight was to be in an Italian-built *N-1* airship, to be named *Norge*, for Norway, but to be captained by its Italian designer-pilot, Nobile. Duly *Norge* arrived in Spitzbergen. Meanwhile the American aviator, Commander Byrd, arrived too, with two aeroplanes, a large Fokker and *Josephine Ford*. When there seemed to be no room for his ship to dock at King's Bay alongside a ship partly occupied by the Amundsen/Nobile party, Byrd resourcefully floated his aircraft ashore, lashed to a pontoon. Hearing that the Byrd/Bennett team might manage to get off the ground for the Pole first, Nobile tried to hurry on preparations for a premature departure of *Norge*, but Amundsen would have none of it. An unplanned dash was not his style. Overnight, the rival 'ships', so entirely different in design, stood scarcely 200 yards apart. Then Byrd was off in his heavier-than-air *Josephine Ford* at two o'clock in the morning, to return triumphant at five in the afternoon. Amundsen and Ellsworth both declared themselves delighted; flying over the Pole (they stoutly maintained) was only *one* of their own projects. Nevertheless, it must have been an ironic experience for the man who had won the land race to the South Pole to be pipped at the air post for the North.

When *Norge* finally took off with Amundsen and Nobile, plus Nobile's little dog, Titina, on 11 May, there was another ludicrous scene. Amundsen and Ellsworth had each brought a small flag, 'not much larger than a pocket handkerchief', to drop over the Pole. Not so their pilot: 'Imagine our astonishment to see Nobile dropping overside not one, but armfuls, of flags,' said Amundsen. 'The *Norge* looked like a circus wagon of the skies.' Nobile produced one Italian national banner so huge he could hardly stuff it out through the window. When he did, it clung to the side of the front gondola before ripping back to the rear gondola, threatening to foul the propeller. At length, at least five miles

Opposite Amundsen would have no truck with horses. He decided to take dogs, for two reasons. They were to pull sledges loaded with provisions. Then, when provisions were exhausted, the sledges would be abandoned and the dogs themselves be eaten.

Right When their ponies collapsed, Scott and his party were forced to haul sledges loaded with stores over the Beardmore Glacier. In bad weather such exertions proved too much for them.

Right Scott with his men at the South Pole: 'Great God! This is an awful place, and terrible enough for us to have laboured to it without the reward of priority,' he wrote.

Opposite The triumph of Amundsen and his men at the South Pole. 'The sledging was ideal and the weather beautiful,' he wrote. 'We have never had to move a foot; all we had to do was let ourselves be towed along.'

beyond the Pole, 'it fluttered free and sank swiftly to the surface of the ice below us'.

Yet when Nobile was in trouble in 1928 in another dirigible, the *Italia*, which had crashed in the Arctic, Amundsen came out of retirement to volunteer to search for him. 'Ah, if you only knew how splendid it is up there!' he said to his friend Giudici. 'That's where I want to die; and I only wish that death will come to me chivalrously.' Nobile's feeble wireless messages had been heard by a Russian farmer. Amundsen took off from Tromsoe, for the first leg of his flight to Spitzbergen, in a Latham seaplane. Meanwhile Nobile himself – once again, inseparable from his dog – was found and rescued. But of Amundsen there was no sign until a pontoon from the Latham was seen floating in the sea off the Fugloe Isles, ten weeks later. Amundsen's last wish had been granted: he died trying to save a man he scorned.

Out of Their Element

The *Apollo 11* Moon Landing

1 16 July 1969. Armstrong, Aldrin and Collins take off from Cape Kennedy on top of the giant Apollo 11 vehicle. After only minutes the *Saturn V* first stage and the *Saturn II* second stage have dropped away. The *Saturn IVB* third stage boosts the astronauts into earth orbit and later on towards the moon.

2 The lunar lander is removed from the spent *IVB* by the command and service module.

3 The command, service and lunar modules rotate slowly in space in order to equalize temperatures on their journey to the moon.

4 After orientation, the service module rocket decelerates all three modules into lunar orbit. Collins remains in the command and service modules (*Columbia*). Aldrin and Armstrong transfer to the lunar lander (*Eagle*) which then separates and begins the descent to Tranquillity Base on the moon's surface.

5 After lunar exploration Aldrin and Armstrong take off in the top half of *Eagle*. Collins aboard *Columbia* has been monitoring their work from lunar orbit. *Columbia* and *Eagle* dock. All three astronauts meet aboard *Columbia* and, after jettisoning *Eagle* on to the surface of the moon as an experiment in lunar seismometry, accelerate out of orbit and towards earth.

6 The command module separates from the service module, which is jettisoned. The astronauts turn the command module round to present their retarding shield to the earth's atmosphere. Collins, Armstrong and Aldrin parachute to the Pacific for splashdown aboard the command module, the only part of the giant vehicle to return to earth in one piece. They are picked up by a US Navy aircraft carrier.

Tranquillity Base

20 July 1969. Aldrin and Armstrong explore Tranquillity Base. Armstrong collects lunar rock samples, Aldrin checks a moonquake recorder (seismometer), which will record the impact of the ascent stage of *Eagle* after its jettison from orbit.
Between Aldrin and Eagle: laser reflector for measuring earth–moon distance.
Behind Eagle: strip collector for measuring solar wind and earth-linked television camera.

Tranquillity Base

Above Jacques-Yves Cousteau's *soucoupe plongeante* (diving saucer) can move about under water as desired. By developing the aqualung with Emile Gagnan, Cousteau at last freed the diver to go about his work without trailing pipes and cords.

Opposite Earth, as seen from the moon.

Unlike the sailing ship, which wove a pattern of wind against wave, wave against wind, across the oceans of the world, the balloon could only float at the mercy of the breeze. Would-be balloonist-explorers were handicapped by being unable to control anything much except ascent and descent. Only a heavier-than-air machine could choose its own direction, either by copying a winged bird – which was what Leonardo da Vinci attempted in his sketches – or by creating an artificial turbulence which would force air to flow over inclinable planes and thus provide lift and fall, as well as movement from side to side. Of the many pioneers and enthusiasts of what now seem outrageously dangerous machines, the Wright brothers were the first to succeed, on any real scale, in turning a glider into an aeroplane with the help of an engine. In 1903 they managed to stay aloft for fifty-nine seconds; two years later they managed half an hour and travelled twenty-four and a half miles. A new era had begun.

Explorers would soon test the new machines to their limits, by adding power, petrol tanks and increasingly sophisticated devices. Gradually, though man was still important, the emphasis shifted from the flier to the techniques of flying. One of those alive to what was happening was Amundsen; he told Nansen how glad he was to have been born early enough to become an old-style explorer: 'In future there will be nothing to go for but the moon.' He had seen for himself, during the aerial race for the Pole, how the whole basis of exploration had been changed. In the future, why trudge painfully to some hitherto unknown corner of the world if you could fly over it? In 1933 Lord Clydesdale did just that, flying twice over Mount Everest, the highest point on earth, and took photographs to prove it. The flight also demonstrated that climbers of Everest would need to be artificially sustained by oxygen packs on their backs.

The air, to an extent, was now navigable,

oxygen on their backs and lightweight suits, divers could now reach depths of 200 feet, and scientific research of the ocean's depths was thus greatly extended. But as divers descended further into the depths, so the dangers of the 'bends' (decompression sickness, caused by bubbles of nitrogen forming in the blood as the diver returns to the surface) were increased. In 1957 research into decompression sickness came up with the finding that a helium-oxygen mixture ensures self-decompression, and one more danger was removed.

A lone, unprotected diver remains extremely vulnerable, however, and to descend to greater depths diving bells, bathyscaphes and submarines were developed. In 1960 Jacques Piccard reached the bottom of the seven-mile-deep Mariana Trench in the Pacific, in the bathyscaphe *Trieste*; and a nuclear submarine, the USS *Nautilus*, in 1958 made one of the most exciting undersea journeys ever undertaken, travelling from the Pacific to the Atlantic beneath the North Pole.

The five continents of the world are now known; inaccessible areas can be charted from the air, and deep-sea laboratories are exploring the oceans' depths. But, until only twenty years ago, a vast area remained unexplored: space.

On 4 October 1957 the Russians launched *Sputnik I* into orbit around the earth; they followed it up with *Sputnik II*, which could not return to earth, but which nevertheless contained a living passenger, the dog Laika, wired up to transmit her body's reactions back to scientists on earth. The chimpanzee Ham was NASA's answer to Laika. A *Redstone* missile took off into space to return after a few minutes, with Ham still alive. Two months later, on 12 April 1961, the Russians sent out Yuri Gagarin, the first man to go into orbit, re-enter the earth's atmosphere and bump down on land. The Americans preferred splashdowns at sea. The race was on and it took a peculiar form; for the ostensible object was to be the first to land a man on the moon – bringing him back safely – yet one of the main reasons for American keenness was the belief (wholly justified) that American technology could beat Russian technology on a project of such enormous popular appeal. The hope was realized by employing a most complex system of machines (rockets in disposable stages to carry a space-craft and a lunar module into orbit round the moon) for a descent, controlled from far-away earth, of

Above Yuri Gagarin, the Russian astronaut who was the first man to go into orbit round the earth.

Top Jacques Piccard in the bathyscaphe *Trieste*, which descended seven miles to the floor of the Pacific Ocean.

but the ocean floors remained unconquered. Without oxygen equipment sea exploration was limited to the length of time a man could hold his breath. Men had long laboured to solve the problem; Leonardo da Vinci produced drawings of a diving suit, but it was not until 1838 that the first diving suits came into regular use. In 1942 came the breakthrough of the aqualung, developed by Jacques Cousteau and Emile Gagnan. With a supply of the module to the moon's surface. In July 1969, whilst Michael Collins stayed aloft, Neil Armstrong and Buzz Aldrin in their module *Eagle* bumped gently onto their chosen landing-site in the Sea of Tranquillity. 'The *Eagle* has landed!' they shouted jubilantly. Six hours later the hatch opened and Armstrong set first human foot on the moon. 'One small step for man, one giant leap for mankind.' The Stars and Stripes were unfurled and a plaque set up: 'WE CAME IN PEACE FOR ALL MANKIND.'

They had come as a result of the skill of the scientists who had designed machinery to put them there. They stayed because their superbly-constructed space-suits ensured that earth's atmosphere and pressure were carried about with them wherever they went. Unable to support human life,

the moon was a dead place, cratered as much by bombardment from outer space as from internal eruptions, airless and dusty.

The sophisticated technology which took *Apollo XI* to the moon may yet take men to other planets, and unmanned probes have already been sent to Mars, Venus, Jupiter and Saturn. From their capsules astronauts can see the whole surface of the globe, whose geography we now know well. However, we have travelled in space as little as the people of medieval Europe had travelled outside the Mediterranean lands. Technology has helped to reveal the secrets of the earth's surface; it may now herald the beginning of a new era of exploration. But whatever may be found out there, it is safe to say that man's curiosity will remain as boundless as before.

Below Eagle at Tranquillity Base. Neil Armstrong's footprints can be clearly seen on the powdery surface of the moon.

Acknowledgments

The author wishes to acknowledge his debt to the chief librarian and staff at the Royal Geographical Society library for their invaluable help whilst consulting literally hundreds of books by authors past and present, including the learned contributors to *Encyclopaedia Britannica*. Of all these authors, if one alone should be selected, then it must be Sir Percy Sykes for the many instalments of *The Story of Exploration and Adventure*. Heartfelt thanks also to Tom Damant, Marina, Gian-Carlo Pasqualetto, Mamma Cesira, Bobby and Marco.

Photographs and illustrations were supplied or are reproduced by kind permission of the following:

Aldus Archives 57, 128
Ardea Photographics 30 (Richard Waller), 59 (Caroline Weaver), 112–13 (Richard Waller), 114, 114–15, 126–7 (Alan Weaving), 130 below (Elizabeth S.Burgess), 152 (Clem Haagner), 157, 168–9 (E.Mickleburgh)
Australia House Reference Library 107
Dr John Baker 129 below (John Gates), 130 above (John Gates)
Barnaby's Picture Library 181
Biblioteca Nazionale, Florence 52 below (Scala)
Bibliothèque Nationale, Paris 1, 28 below (MS Sup. pers. 1113 f.204v)
Black Star, New York 180 above
Bodleian Library, Oxford 11 above, 26 (MS Bodley 264 f.218), 27 (MS Bodley 264 f.239), 29 (MS Bodley 264 f.260), 32 (Pococke 375 ff.3v/4r), 33 below (MS Bodley 264 f.265)
British Museum, London 19, 20, 24 (Robert Harding Associates), 58 below (Werner Forman Archive), 61 (MS Roy.20.E.IX ff.27v/28), 83 (Sloane 197 ff.181v/182), 84–5 (MS Harl.3450 ff.5v/6r), 86, 144
British Museum (Natural History), London 100 right
Cairo Museum 10 (Werner Forman Archive)

Camera Press 34–5 (Wim Swaan)
Alan Cash 90 below
Cavalry and Guards Club 172–3 (Prudence Cuming)
Christies Ltd. 25 above (Cooper-Bridgman)
Denver Public Library, Western History Dept. 68, 69 below
Deutschen Akademie der Wissenschaften zu Berlin, East Berlin 72–3 (Robert Harding Associates/Gerard Reinhold)
Edinburgh University Library 31 (MS Arab 20 f.4)
Werner Forman Archive 46, 60 above, 81
Fram Museum, Oslo 174 below
Geoslides 4–5
Gilcrease Institute 67, 69 above, 70 above and below
Robert Harding Associates 7, 21 (Saisoon), 28 above (John Massey Steward), 55 (Robert Cundy), 71, 117 (Patrick Matthews), 121 (Yoram Lehmann), 134 below, 135 (Watts)
Wally Herbert Collection 163 (Robert Harding Associates)
Michael Holford 11 below
John Judkyn Memorial Museum, Bath 53 below (Aldus Archives)
Illustrated London News 175 below
Collection of the Duke of Infantado 56 (Mas)
Graham Keen 37 below
Kunsthistorisches Museum, Vienna 17
Mansell Collection 54, 64, 137, 171
Pierpont Morgan Library 85 (Aldus Archives)
Museo de America, Madrid 58 above (Mas)
Museo Historico Regionál del Cuzco, Peru 60 below (Aldus Archives)
Nasjonalgalleriet, Oslo 48 above (O.Vaering)
National Library of Australia, Rex Nan Kivell Collection 92 (Aldus Archives)
National Maritime Museum, Greenwich 2–3, (on loan from Ministry of Defence) 50–1, (Rodney Todd-White), 64–5 (Rodney Todd-White), 63, 88–9, 91, 96 (Greenwich Hospital Collection), 97 above (on loan from Ministry of Defence) and below, 98–9, 100 left, 101, 147, 150–1

National Portrait Gallery, London 62, 66, 113, 118 left and right, 132, 148 above, 153 above
New York Historical Society 87
Novosti Press Agency 180 below
Popperfoto 170 below, 175 above
Radio Times Hulton Picture Library 165, 167 below, 174 above
Les Réquins Associés, Neuilly 179
London Borough of Richmond upon Thames 122 above, 122 below (John Gates)
Rijksmuseum, Amsterdam 94 below (Aldus Archives)
Library of the Royal Commonwealth Society 102, 103, 104 above and below
Royal Geographical Society endpapers, 40, 74 above, 93 below, 108 below, 123, 127, 129 above, 131, 134 above, 141 above, 149 above, 154 above, 164, 164–5, 166, 167 above
Christopher Scarlett 22–3, 36 above, 37 above
Science Museum, London (Crown Copyright) 53 above
Scottish Tourist Board 12
Statens Historiska Museet, Stockholm 47 (Werner Forman Archive), 48 below
Topkapi Palace, Istanbul 33 above
United Society for the Propagation of the Gospel 132–3
Uffizi Gallery, Florence 52 above (Scala)
Viking Ships Museum, Oslo 49 (Werner Forman Archive)
ZEFA 25 below (J.Bitsch), 38–9 (J.Bitsch), 106 (D.Baglin), 108 above (D.Baglin), 109 (R.Halin), 116 (J.Ibach)

Maps by David Worth and Jennifer Mexter

All possible care has been taken in tracing the ownership of any copyright material used in this book and in making acknowledgment for its use. If any owner has not been acknowledged the publishers apologize and will be glad of the opportunity to rectify the error.

Index